THE EPISTLE TO THE ROMANS

EPWORTH PREACHER'S COMMENTARIES

*

THE EPISTLE TO THE ROMANS

*

VINCENT TAYLOR
D.D., F.B.A.

LONDON : THE EPWORTH PRESS

Book Steward
FRANK H. CUMBERS

SET IN MONOTYPE TIMES ROMAN AND PRINTED IN
GREAT BRITAIN BY THE CAMELOT PRESS LTD
LONDON AND SOUTHAMPTON

General Introduction

WE are living in a day in which the authority and message of the Bible are being re-discovered and declared. Preachers are realizing afresh that their message must be based on the Word of God in Scripture. Many commentaries on the books of the Bible are already available, and give much space to the consideration of critical questions and historical and literary problems.

This new series of commentaries, as its name suggests, is written specifically for preachers, and particularly for those who feel themselves ill-equipped to study the more advanced works of scholarship. Its aim is to set forth the essential message of the Bible. Questions of authorship, date, background, etc., will be dealt with briefly, and only in so far as they are necessary for informed preaching. The main purpose of each commentary will be (a) to explain the original meaning of each Biblical passage, and (b) to indicate its relevance to human need in the present situation. Bearing in mind this dual purpose, each author will have freedom to use what method of treatment he thinks most suitable to the book of the Bible on which he is commenting.

To save space, the Biblical text is not printed, but the commentary is based on that of the *Revised Version*.

Our intention is to publish two commentaries each year, one on an Old Testament book, one on a New Testament book, and at a moderate price.

This first volume of the *Epworth Preacher's Commentaries*, on *Romans*, is written by Dr Vincent Taylor, one of the most eminent New Testament scholars of our day, who makes his own distinctive contribution to the series.

GREVILLE P. LEWIS

Preface

THIS commentary is an attempt to elucidate Paul's meaning in what by wide consent is the most important of his Epistles. In agreement with the Series to which it belongs, it is intended primarily for the use of preachers and of general readers who are interested in the Apostle's teaching. For this reason, it is based upon the English Revised Version, although naturally I have had the Greek text constantly in mind.

Each section of the Epistle is preceded by a brief paraphrase or summary and is followed by a paragraph in which the principal themes are indicated and in some cases discussed. I have not attempted to supply outlines for sermons, being convinced that the chief service one can give to preachers is to explain what Paul says as accurately as possible. It is for the preacher himself to decide how he will treat any theme which may commend itself to him, giving it a modern setting and applying its message to present-day needs by his knowledge of literature, history, life, and religious experience. Having read the Epistle for many years with students, I am convinced that it has a vital message for readers today, especially for those who are tired of trivial themes and wish to examine the central truths of the gospel.

While I am deeply indebted to the standard commentaries of Sanday and Headlam, J. Denney, G. G. Findlay, C. A. Anderson Scott, P. C. Boylan, C. H. Dodd, K. Kirk, J. Knox, and other writers, I have not felt able to afford space to discuss the opinions of others. This lack will account, I hope, for an unavoidable categorical element in some of the comments, especially as brevity and directness are essential to my purpose. Within these limits, however, I have not failed to indicate points where different opinions are held. Some explanation of the difficulties which confront the general reader is appended below, and with hesitation I have offered a glossary of the principal Pauline words which are familiar to students, but are difficult or obscure for the general reader. I have written this commentary in the hope that it may prove useful in the exposition of one of the greatest writings in Christian literature, a touchstone of faith and a fire of hope.

ST ANNES ON SEA
31st January 1955

VINCENT TAYLOR

Preface to the Second Edition

I AM glad to find that after the lapse of six years there is a need for a Second Edition of this little commentary on *Romans*. I welcome this need because for some time I have felt that the first edition was too brief and concise, with the result that important points did not receive the attention they deserved. In this edition some attempt is made to overcome this defect. The opportunity to do this is all the more welcome since I have been able to profit from commentaries on *Romans* written since 1955, including those of C. K. Barrett and F. J. Leenhardt published in 1957 and 1960, and also from some of the renderings in the *New English Bible*. I trust that in its new form my commentary will continue to meet a need in the Series to which it belongs.

30th September 1961   VINCENT TAYLOR

Contents

Questions of Introduction to the Epistle

THE Epistle consists of five unequal parts: (1) An introductory section, 1^{1-17}; (2) the main doctrinal section which treats of the Righteousness of God by Faith, 1^{18}-8^{39}; (3) a discussion of the question of God's Purpose for Jew and Gentile, 9^1-11^{36}; (4) a hortatory section describing Life in the New Age made possible by the Righteousness of God, 12^1-15^{13}; and (5) Concluding Explanations and Greetings, 15^{14}-16^{27}.

Genuineness of the Epistle

That the Epistle was written by Paul is undisputed save by an extreme Dutch school of critics. It was known and used by Clement of Rome (c. A.D. 95), Ignatius (c. A.D. 110), and Justin Martyr (c. A.D. 150), and it is expressly quoted by the second-century Fathers, Irenaeus and Clement of Alexandria.

Date and Purpose of the Epistle

Paul is on the point of going to Jerusalem '*ministering to the saints*' there. Later he proposes to visit Rome on his way to Spain ($15^{19, 25, 28}$). He writes to restate the leading principles of his gospel in the light of his experience and with a view to his further missionary labours.

The Epistle was written from Corinth in A.D. 56 or 57.

The First Readers

Probably the Church at Rome consisted of a Gentile Christian majority ($1^{5-6, 13-14}$, 11^{13}, 15^{15-16}) with a Jewish Christian nucleus (4^1, 9^{10}, 7^1). Several features suggest that, in addition to its Roman form, the letter was edited for a wider circle (by the omission of 'in Rome' in $1^{7, 15}$ and of 15^1-16^{23}, and by the addition of 16^{25-7}). There is no reason to question the authenticity of any part of the Epistle, save 16^{25-7}, but 15^{14-33} and 16^{1-23} may be portions of separate Pauline letters. Some scholars think that 16^{1-23} was written by the Apostle to commend Phœbe to the Church at Ephesus, but others think that its Roman destination is more probable.

Abiding Value

The importance of the Epistle cannot be exaggerated. Its immense influence on Luther is well known, and it was while one was reading Luther's Preface to the Epistle at Aldersgate Street that John Wesley's heart was 'strangely warmed'. Today its value is in no way diminished. Whenever the vitality of the Church is low, men turn to the Epistle to the Romans. 'There has been no religious revival within Christianity, that has not been, on one side at least, a return to St Paul' (Dean Inge).

The Interpretation of the Epistle

ALTHOUGH there are many passages in *Romans* which taken by themselves are immediately clear, as, for example, 6^{12-23}, 8^{1-15}, 12, and 14^{13-23}, it cannot be said that the argument of the whole is easy to follow and understand. It may, therefore, be of advantage to point out where the difficulties lie and how they may be overcome.

First, the profundity of the Apostle's thought must be mentioned. Paul deals with the deepest things in the Christian revelation and experience, the purposes of God, election, justification, salvation past and present, and the central theme which unites the whole, the righteousness of God, itself a truth not readily understood. All these things have to be examined closely, if the Epistle is to convey its full message.

Secondly, the brilliance of the Apostle's literary style has to be recognized. Paul often writes under the stress of deep emotion, leaving not a little to be supplied by the intelligent reader. This fact accounts for the obscurity of passages like 5^{16-18}, 8^3, and 12^{6-8}. He is also fond of epigrams like those in 11^{32} and 14^{23b}, and of playing upon words as in $6^{18,\ 20-2}$. He expects a good deal from his readers and is not afraid of being misunderstood.

Thirdly, as might be expected, he writes against the background of the thought of his day in respect of such matters as the law, circumcision, racial solidarity, supernatural powers, and the like. These ideas cannot be taken in the reader's stride. They have to be understood and related to modern ways of thinking.

Fourthly, and in particular, Paul's use of the Old Testament is that of his time. The modern reader, if in any way he has been schooled in the exposition of the Old Testament, asks what the psalmist or the prophet quoted intended to say to the people of his own day. Paul is not interested in such matters. He reads the ancient scriptures with deep insight, but does not hesitate to put his own interpretation upon what he reads. This habit raises real difficulties when the argument turns on Old Testament passages, as, for example, Hab 2^4 quoted in 1^{17} and Gen 15^6 in 4^3, and also when he finds significance in the fact that one passage precedes another in order, Gen 15^6 concerning faith counted for righteousness and Gen 17^{11} which mentions circumcision. He does not always introduce his formula of quotation 'according as it is written', and sometimes uses the words of scripture as the vehicle of his own thought, as in 10^{6-8}. Nor does he feel it necessary to quote the Old

Testament with exactitude. The modern reader of the Epistle needs to familiarize himself with Paul's methods, or want of methods, and has to resist the temptation to expect the Apostle to use scripture as he himself thinks it should be used. The desire to express Paul's thoughts in modern forms is praiseworthy, but it must not lead us to attempt to modernize the Apostle himself. A Christian, he is also a child of contemporary Judaism.

Fifthly, the most serious difficulty is the necessary limitations of Paul's psychological terminology. Paul knows much about instincts, complexes, sentiments, conflict, and sublimation, but it would be ridiculous to expect him to use anything like modern psychological jargon. Moreover, the terms he does use all need to be understood, 'body', 'flesh', 'mind', in particular. Adjustment in this matter on the part of the modern reader is not easy, for he is inclined to put his own meaning upon these expressions, a meaning which may not be that of Paul himself. Some account of the more difficult Pauline terms is given in the Glossary printed below. But the warning must be given that we cannot find a single English equivalent for each Pauline expression, for Paul himself does not consistently use each one in the same sense. This means that each example of the use of these terms has to be examined and considered in its own context. It also explains why even the best commentators differ in their interpretations.

All the considerations mentioned above demand that the reader of *Romans* must bring to his task knowledge as well as intelligence. Mere rapid reading is not without value, but it is of strictly limited value. Paul asks from us the best that we can give, and to those who give freely he imparts from his treasures 'the unsearchable riches of Christ'.

Glossary

ONLY general guidance is attempted in this Glossary, since the terms selected for comment need in all cases to be studied in their immediate contexts.

Body. This is one of the most difficult terms used in *Romans*, for while the body (or *soma*) is often the physical body, it is significant that on occasion Paul feels it necessary to characterize it as the 'mortal body' (6^{12}, 8^{11}). The key to Paul's usage is the fact that, unlike the Greeks, the Jews did not think of the body as the sheath or envelope of the soul, from which it is freed at death, but as part of the human personality without which the latter is incomplete. Sometimes Paul uses the word of 'the person' or 'self' as in 12^1, and sometimes of what might be called 'the lower self', as in 7^{24}, and $8^{10, 13}$, and again of 'the sinful self'. In 12^5 it is used of the Christian community, the Church, though probably not in 7^4.

Death. The term is naturally used of physical death in 1^{32}, 5^{10}, and 6^{10}, and 7^5 but it is probably used of spiritual death in $7^{10, 13, 24}$ and $8^{2, 6}$. A striking feature of Paul's usage is his use of Death as a demonic tyrannical power in $5^{12, 14, 17, 21}$, 7^{23}, and 8^{38}.

Faith. Paul employs the word 'faith' and the verb 'to believe' to describe dependence upon God in Christ, trust in Him, and reliance upon His saving activity.

Flesh. 'Flesh' (*sarx*), like 'body' (*soma*), is a particularly difficult word, for it is not used of material flesh, but of human nature in its various aspects. The phrase 'according to the flesh' means 'humanly speaking' or 'from the human standpoint' (cf. 1^3, 4^1, and $9^{3, 5}$), and Paul actually uses 'my flesh' in 11^{14} to designate his kinsmen. In 3^{20} it has the meaning 'man', and in 6^{19} and 9^8 it describes human nature in its frailty. Frequently in *Romans* it denotes the lower self-centred nature of man dominated by sin (cf. $7^{5, 18, 25}$, 8^{3-13}, and 13^{14}). In these passages it is not suggested that human nature is inherently evil, but that in it sin has established its seat.

Justification. 'Justification' is the action of God in declaring men righteous, in treating them as such, and in putting them right with Himself. It is not the act or process of being made righteous. In this respect it differs from sanctification. Surprisingly enough,

Paul uses the noun rarely, only twice (4²⁵ and 5¹⁸) in *Romans* and not at all in *Galatians*. He prefers to use the verb 'to justify', which he uses twenty-five times in *Romans*, *Galatians*, and *1 Corinthians*. The condition of justification is faith, in the sense defined above, and its ground or basis is the atoning work of Christ. It is not 'by works' or anything man can do that he is justified, but 'by faith' alone (cf. 4⁵). I have discussed the relationship between Justifying Faith and Righteousness and the place of Justification in modern theology in *Forgiveness and Reconciliation* (pp. 55-69).

Heart. In both the OT and the NT 'heart' is much wider in meaning than in English usage. It is not only the seat of feeling (cf. 9², 10¹), but also of the mind or understanding (1²¹), and indeed the whole personality (5⁵, 8²⁷, 10¹⁰). So also in the teaching of Jesus (cf. Mk 2⁸, 12³⁰, &c.).

Law. Usually by 'Law' Paul means the Mosaic Law, but in a number of cases he appears to mean 'law in general' or 'the legal principle'. Not unnaturally commentators differ in interpreting the relevant passages.

Mind. 'Mind' is the term used by Paul to denote the higher rational element in man, the 'inner' or 'inmost self' (cf. 7²³, ²⁵, 12², and 14⁵). In 1²⁸ the 'base mind' is mentioned and in 11³⁴ the 'mind' of the Lord.

Reconciliation. 'Reconciliation' is God's act in restoring men to fellowship with Himself, the healing of broken relationships. The noun is used in 5¹¹ and 11¹⁵ and the corresponding verb in 5¹⁰.

Righteousness. 'Righteousness' is a key word in *Romans*. It is found there no less than thirty-four times. 'Righteousness' is frequently used to describe man's right standing with God (4³⁻⁶, ⁹, ²², 6¹³, ¹⁶, 10³⁻⁴, ¹⁰, 14¹⁷, etc.), and in this respect 'the righteousness which is of the law' (10⁵) is distinguished from 'the righteousness of faith' (4¹³, 9³⁰, 10⁶, etc.) which is almost an equivalent expression for 'justification'. The phrase 'the righteousness of God' (1¹⁷, 3⁵, ²¹⁻²) or 'His righteousness' (3²⁵⁻⁶) is especially important. It describes, not so much a quality which He possesses, but His saving activity, His action in justifying men and so bringing them into right relationships with Himself.

Sin. Sin in Paul's Epistles, as in the New Testament generally, is disobedience to, or rebellion against, God. It is self coronation. Frequently, however, as in his use of 'death', Paul personifies sin, and represents it as a demonic power which reigns in the world and in the heart of man (cf. 5¹²⁻¹³, ²¹, 6¹²⁻²³, 7⁹⁻¹⁴, and 8³). He also speaks of it, as the Rabbis did, as an evil inclination set within the heart.

Soul. The word is not frequently found in *Romans* where the commonest expressions for the 'self' are 'mind', 'flesh', 'spirit', and 'body'. 'Soul' is used in the sense of 'life' in 11^3 and 16^4, and with the meaning 'man' in 13^1. Cf. 2^9, 'Every soul of man'. These four are the only examples of the use of the word in the Epistle.

Spirit. Predominantly used of the Holy Spirit, 'spirit' is also used of the 'higher' or 'divine self' in 1^9, $8^{10, \ 16}$, and in 12^{11} ('fervent in spirit') unless here the Holy Spirit is meant.

An Outline of the Epistle

I The Introduction

II The Righteousness of God by Faith

III God's Purposes for Jew and Gentile

B

IV Life in the New Age made possible by God's Righteous Activity

V   Concluding Explanations and Greetings

Abbreviations

AV—Authorized Version.
RV—Revised Version.
RSV—Revised Standard Version.
NEB—New English Bible.

The Use of the Epistle in Preaching

How may one use the Epistle to the Romans in preaching? This question is not easy to answer. How can one base sermons on a letter written long ago by a writer with a different outlook in a very different world situation? The need for a Glossary shows that he uses key words in a peculiar sense. As we have already seen, his psychological terms are not ours; his use of the Old Testament is strange to us; and many of his problems appear to be those of another age. It is not surprising therefore that as a rule *Romans* is not a preacher's first choice. What in these circumstances must he do?

The first thing to do is to disregard preaching and to study closely the Epistle itself. What does Paul mean? What is he trying to say? We must not read it 'with a view to sermons', but in order to understand its message. The diligent study of the Scriptures is an indispensable approach to preaching. As Paul himself writes, 'All the ancient scriptures were written for our own instruction, in order that through the encouragement they give us we may maintain our hope with fortitude' (15⁴, *NEB*). He was thinking of the Old Testament, but what he says is true also of the New.

Once we become familiar with Paul's use of words, his psychological ideas, and his special problems, we begin to realize how modern he is. We are like the man who, on hearing the first chapter of *Romans* read to a Chinese crowd, is said to have cried, 'He is reading about us'.

The basic assumption of the letter is that by reason of his self-trust and confidence man is alienated from God and that, in consequence, he falls under His judgement. As Scripture testifies this is the state of all men. Man is a sinner. 'All alike have sinned, and are deprived of the divine splendour' (3²³, *NEB*). This teaching describes our modern situation. What else can be said by any one who looks around upon the world of today? No less relevant is Paul's claim that man cannot save himself from this situation by his own efforts to fulfil any legal code. 'By the works of the law shall no flesh be justified in his sight: for through the law comes the know-ledge of sin' (3²⁰). Man cannot save himself. But God can and will. It is as much 'good news' today, as it was when Paul first wrote, that God has revealed a way of 'putting men right with Himself'. By His sacrificial death Christ covers or expiates sin, and through faith in Him men obtain a new standing with God, peace with Him, and hope in His glory. 'God's free gift is eternal life in union with Christ Jesus our Lord' (6²³, *NEB*).

Once we have penetrated to the centre of Paul's thought, themes for preaching emerge on every side—Christ's life-giving power, the gift of the Spirit who aids our prayer and speaks for us, our security in the love of God from which nothing can separate us, God's ultimate purposes for man, life within the Christian community, its privileges and its responsibilities. These are some of the more outstanding examples of Paul's message for us today. In brooding over his letter we discover that his theology is a preacher's treasury.

ONE

The Introduction to the Epistle

THE Introduction consists of two parts: (1) 1^{1-7}, the opening Salutation; (2) 1^{8-17}, Paul and his Readers, The Theme of the Epistle.

(1) 1^{1-7}: The Opening Salutation

In this section Paul describes himself as '*the slave of Christ Jesus*', as '*called to be an apostle*', and as '*separated unto the gospel of God*'. This gospel, he insists, is no new thing for it is rooted in the Old Testament in the promises made through the prophets, and it has its centre in God's Son. On the human side He was a descendant of David, but on the divine side He was marked out as the Son of God with power by the resurrection from the dead. He is '*Jesus Christ our Lord*'. It was through Him, Paul declares, that he himself received grace and the office of an Apostle, with a view to that obedience which springs from faith, a commission to be fulfilled among the Gentiles on His behalf. Among these the readers are included. It is to all of them in Rome that he writes, and he salutes them in the words: '*Grace to you and peace from God our Father and the Lord Jesus Christ*.'

1^1. '*a servant of Jesus Christ*', or, more literally, 'a slave of Jesus Christ'. This phrase, which recalls Mark 10^{44}, '*Whosoever would be first among you, shall be servant* (RVm, "*bondservant*") *of all*', is appreciated if we remember the wide prevalence of slavery in the Roman Empire. It is used deliberately by Paul of himself (cf. Gal 1^{10}, Phil 1^1) and of others (cf. 1 Cor 7^1, Col 4^{12}, Eph 6^6). Christ Himself, it was remembered, '*took the form of a slave*' (Phil 2^7).

'*called to be an apostle*'. An emphasis on election, or calling, is characteristic of the Epistle. See 1^{6-7}, 8^{28-9}.

'*separated*', that is 'set apart'. Paul is deeply conscious of the fact that he has been set apart by God for the work of proclaiming the gospel.

'*the gospel of God*', the good news about God and His gift

in Christ. But '*of God*' may mean that God is the source of the good news. See Barrett, 17f. See further **1¹⁶**. Paul has the noun 56 times.

1². '*which he promised afore by his prophets*'. It is a pronounced feature of Paul's thought that, although the good news is new in point of time, it is closely linked with the message of the Old Testament prophets.

'*the holy scriptures*'. Normally (4³, 9¹⁷, 10²², 11², Gal 3⁸, ²², 4³⁰) Paul uses the singular noun, except here and 15⁴, 16²⁶ and 1 Cor 15³⁻⁴. With the first Christians Paul attached the greatest importance to the fact that the gospel was grounded in the ancient promises of God. Cf. Acts 2¹⁴⁻³⁶, 3¹²⁻²⁶, etc.

1³. '*concerning his Son*' marks the centre of '*the gospel of God*'. For '*his Son*' see also **1⁹, 5¹⁰, 8²⁹**; '*his own Son*', **8³, ³²**; '*the Son of God*', **1⁴**.

'*according to the flesh*' (cf. **9⁵**), 'on the physical side', 'as far as physical descent is concerned'.

'*born of the seed of David*', an accepted belief in the primitive Church.

1⁴. '*declared to be*', or, better, 'designated'.

'*with power*' should be taken with 'designated'.

'*according to the spirit of holiness*'. The phrase is explained by very many commentators as a reference to the Holy Spirit, but the parallel with '*according to the flesh*' suggests that it refers to Christ's spirit or person in its holiness. This distinction, however, is probably too subtle in a statement which appears to rest upon a primitive creed or confession. The balanced phrases (in the Greek), 'being born . . . being designated', 'according to . . . according to', 'from . . . from', have a liturgical ring. It seems best, therefore, to conclude that the Holy Spirit is meant.

'*by the resurrection of the dead*'. It would be at variance with Paul's Christology (see **8³**, Phil 2⁶) to suppose that he means that Christ *became* the Son of God at, or in virtue of, the resurrection. The resurrection designated Him as such (cf. Acts 5³¹). An earlier and more naïve Christology may be implied, but not the Adoptionism of later times.

'*our Lord*'. 'Lord' is the most frequent and distinctive name for Christ used by Paul. Its primitive Christian character is illustrated by the Aramaic phrase in 1 Cor 16^{22}, '*Marana tha*' ('Our Lord, come!'). The name was current in contemporary Greek religion with reference to the divinities of the mystery-religions (cf. 1 Cor 8$^{5-6}$). In a papyrus document of the second century we read: 'Chæremon requests your company at dinner at the table of the Lord Sarapis in the Serapæum tomorrow, the 15th, at 9 o'clock.' Current usage may well have fostered the use of the name, but its origin in Christianity is due ultimately to Mark 12$^{35-7}$ and to the impact of the resurrection. See further, Vincent Taylor, *The Names of Jesus*, pp. 38-51. The earliest Christian creed is '*Jesus is Lord*' (cf **10^9**, 1 Cor 12^3).

1^5. '*through whom we received grace and apostleship*'. Paul affirms that he had received his apostolic commission directly from Jesus Christ. Cf. Galatians 1^1, 'Paul, an apostle (not from men, neither through man, but through Jesus Christ and God the Father, who raised him from the dead)'. '*Grace*' translates a word which originally meant 'favour' or 'charm' (cf. Luke 4^{22}). It became a characteristic Christian description of the free unmerited love of God made known in Christ.

'*obedience of faith*', or 'faith-obedience', 'obedience which springs from faith'. It is to promote this that Paul has received grace and apostleship.

'*among all the nations*', better 'Gentiles' (cf. Gal 2^8).

1^7. '*in Rome*' is omitted here (and in **1^{15}**) by some textual authorities, probably because in early times the Epistle was issued for general circulation as well as a letter to Rome.

The beautiful phrase, '*beloved of God, called to be saints*', describes the readers. '*Saints*' are men, not necessarily perfect, who are separated and consecrated to the service of God; cf. also 8^{27}, 12^{13}, 15$^{25f, 31}$, and 16$^{2-15}$. It is important to note that Paul frequently designates believers as '*saints*' or separated men. Contrast the modern meaning of the word to describe holy men canonized or officially recognized by the Church and venerated on earth.

In the salutation the Greek word '*grace*' and the Hebrew '*peace*' are brought together. Note that the name '*the Lord*

'*Jesus Christ*' stands alongside '*God our Father*'. We are so familiar with this usage that we need to remind ourselves that it arose almost at once in the period following the resurrection. It implies the recognition of Christ as divine.

Several themes for preaching are suggested by this section. Paul's Conception of his Mission ('the slave of Christ', called, sent, and dedicated to the service of the gospel); the Nature of the Gospel (rooted in the purposes of God and made known in His Son); the Names of Jesus (Jesus, Christ, Son, Lord); the Marks of a Christian (a slave, beloved of God, called, separated); the New Vocabulary (grace, faith, peace, obedience). '*Called to be saints*' is a text which describes the distinctive nature of the Christian man as (1) called by God for a purpose and therefore known by Him, (2) set apart by God's love, and (3) in consequence, meant to be different (though not by peculiarities) from other men.

(2) 1^{8-17}: Paul and His Readers; the Theme of the Epistle

Paul thanks God '*through Jesus Christ*' for all his readers because their faith is made known throughout the world. He prays for them unceasingly and longs to see them, in order that he may impart to them some spiritual gift to strengthen them, a purpose which he qualifies with the hope that he with them may be encouraged through their mutual faith. He had often purposed to come to them, but had been prevented, his desire being that he might obtain some fruit in them, as among the rest of the Gentiles. He has an obligation both to the Greeks and the barbarians, to the wise and the foolish. Hence his eagerness to preach the gospel to them in Rome. He is not ashamed of the gospel, because it is God's power for salvation, to the Jew first and to the Greek.

The section ends with a statement of the main theme of the Epistle. In the gospel, Paul declares 'God's righteousness is revealed, founded on faith and leading to greater faith', and he supports this statement by a quotation from Hab 2^4: '*The righteous shall live by faith.*'

1^8. Paul's thanksgiving often comes first in his letters. Cf. 1 Thessalonians 1^8. He says '*First*', but is so absorbed in his thought, that he does not add 'secondly' later.

'*your faith is proclaimed throughout the whole world*'. This is not a reference to their Christian belief, but to the distinctive character, and to the moral fruits, of their faith in Christ. They were matters of common knowledge.

1⁹. He calls God to witness ('*God is my witness*'), whom he serves in his spirit in proclaiming the good news, how '*unceasingly*' he prays for his readers, making one request, as he says, in particular.

1¹⁰. '*making request, if by any means now at length, I may be prospered by the will of God to come unto you*'. His longing, as he explains in the next verse, is to impart to them some gift of the Spirit.

'*prospered*'. The same verb is used in 1 Cor 16² and 2 John ². Here it has the meaning of 'being sped on one's way'.

1¹¹. '*some spiritual gift*'. The word 'gift' means a grace-gift, a free gift. This theme is dealt with fully in the section 12⁶⁻⁸.

'*established*', or '*strengthened*'.

1¹². '*comforted*' hardly gives the right idea; 'stirred up' or 'encouraged' is a better rendering. Note that the giving is mutual. Paul believes that he will receive a spiritual gift from the readers as well as imparting one to them, '*each by the other's faith, both yours and mine*'.

1¹³. '*hindered*'. Paul refers to this again in 15²². He had been prevented from coming by his work in Asia Minor and Greece. He had often intended to visit them, but alas! it had not been possible.

1¹⁴. '*I am debtor both to Greeks and Barbarians*'. He is conscious, that is to say, of an obligation to both. By '*Barbarians*' the ancient world meant people strange to Greek culture and speech (cf. Acts 28², ⁴, 1 Cor 14¹¹, Col 3¹¹).

1¹⁵. '*So, as much as in me is, I am ready*'. An awkward, over-literal rendering. A slightly different understanding of the original text suggests the translation, 'Hence my eagerness' (Moffatt).

'*in Rome*'. See the note on **1⁷**.

1¹⁶. '*For I am not ashamed of the gospel*'. A manifest understatement! Actually, he exults in the gospel.

'*for it is the power of God unto salvation*'. This clause strikes the key-note of the letter. Negatively, '*salvation*' is deliverance from sin; positively, it is the attainment of fulness of life. In Paul's teaching the word has both a present and a future (that is, eschatological) significance.

'*to every one that believeth*'. This also is a key-note.

'*to the Jew first*', because the promises of God were made to the Jews, but, as he will maintain, '*also to the Greek*'.

1¹⁷. '*For therein*', that is, in the gospel. The verse is so important theologically speaking in the Epistle that it must be quoted in full. It reads, '*For therein is revealed a righteousness of God by faith unto faith: as it is written, But the righteous shall live by faith*'. The verse is taken up again in **3²¹** after important points vital to Paul's arguments have been treated in **1¹⁸-3²⁰**.

'*a righteousness of God*'. See the Glossary. The phrase indicates an activity of God and not only a quality which He possesses. See C. H. Dodd, *The Epistle to the Romans*, pp. 9-16, also C. K. Barrett, *A Commentary on the Epistle to the Romans*, pp. 17-21.

'*by faith unto faith*'. In Paul's teaching faith is conscious surrender to, and dependence upon, God as revealed in Christ. In saying that '*the righteousness of God*' is '*by faith unto faith*' he means that what God has done must be received by a faith which leads on to a larger and richer faith.

'*as it is written*' (or 'stands written') is Paul's usual formula in referring to the Old Testament.

'*the righteous shall live by faith*'. In Hab 2⁴, from which the quotation is taken, the prophet means that, although menaced by evil, the righteous man lives by his fidelity. Paul puts his own meaning on the passage both here and in Gal 3¹¹. He interprets the words '*by faith*' in the sense of trust in God.

Behind the references to the immediate circumstances we can feel the passionate earnestness which led Paul to be a preacher to the Gentiles (cf. 1 Cor 9¹⁶: '*Woe is me if I preach not the gospel*'). At least three major themes for preaching are suggested by this section, all of which call for explanation to a modern congregation. They are: The Nature of the Gospel (the good news that God's power leads to salvation for every one who receives it in faith, cf. Eph 2⁸); The Righteousness of God (His saving passion, which burns in the Old Testament (cf. Isa 51⁵) and bursts into flame in the Cross of Christ); The Basic Importance of Faith (by which salvation is received, kept, and enriched). It is a delusion to suppose that these themes are not of interest today. Addressed to perennial needs of the human spirit, they have great power if the preacher has studied them in the light of Paul's teaching and has experience of their truth. The text 'Therein a righteousness of God is revealed by faith unto faith' can be treated under the following heads: (1) A Righteousness of God (seen, as explained above, in God's activity in the events of the Exodus and the Return from Babylon), (2) Revealed in the gospel, the same righteous activity in the events of the Crucifixion and the Resurrection, (3) Made Ours by trust in God leading ever throughout the whole of life to a still richer faith. The main thought to urge is that the Christian is the heir to a great heritage, like the men described in the parables of the Hid Treasure (Mt 13[44]) and the Goodly Pearl (Mt 13[45-46]).

TWO

The Righteousness of God by Faith

1^{18}-8^{39}, the main doctrinal part of the Epistle, consists of the following sections: (1) 1^{18}-2^{16}, The Failure of the Gentiles to attain Righteousness; (2) 2^{17}-3^8, The Corresponding Failure of the Jews; (3) $3^{9\text{-}20}$, The Universality of Sin; (4) $3^{21\text{-}31}$, The New Righteousness, Justification by Faith; (5) $4^{1\text{-}25}$, The Example of Abraham's Faith; (6) $5^{1\text{-}11}$, The Results of Justification; (7) $5^{12\text{-}21}$, Christ as the Second Adam; (8) $6^{1\text{-}23}$, Dying to Sin through Union with Christ; (9) $7^{1\text{-}25}$, Freedom from Legal Bondage; (10) $8^{1\text{-}17}$, Life in the Spirit; (11) $8^{18\text{-}30}$, The Glory that is to Be; (12) $8^{31\text{-}9}$, The Certainty of God's Purposes.

(1) 1^{18}-2^{16}: The Failure of the Gentiles to attain Righteousness

(a) $1^{18\text{-}23}$: *The Denial of God*

Paul first describes the reaction of the wrath of God against unrighteous men. What can be known of God, he believes, is made known in the created world, which reveals His everlasting power and divinity. But men, although knowing God, did not honour Him, but became vain and ignorant lapsing into idolatry.

1^{18}. '*the wrath of God*'. This idea is not to be resolved into that of an inevitable process of cause and effect in the moral world; it is the judgement of God Himself upon sinful men both now and hereafter. The wrath is not angry passion, but the condemnation which falls upon sin and sinners in conscious rebellion against God.

'*is revealed*'. The tense is present.

'*ungodliness*' is impiety, defiance of God, and is further a state of mind characterized as '*unrighteousness*' in men who '*hold down*' (or 'suppress') the truth.

1¹⁹. *'that which may be known'*, or possibly 'is known'.
'in them , or 'among them'.

1²⁰. This verse implies the truth of what is called 'Natural Theology', the belief that God makes known His power and divinity in creation, so that men are *'without excuse'*.

1²¹⁻². *'vain in their reasonings'* means that men became frustrated or futile in their thinking. Their minds—for that is what *'heart'* means in biblical language—were *'darkened'*, and contrary to what they themselves imagined, they *'became fools'*.

1²³. The verse describes pagan idolatry. Men *'changed the glory of the incorruptible God for the likeness of an image of corruptible man, and of birds, and fourfooted beasts, and creeping things'*. A terrible indictment!

(b) **1²⁴⁻³²**: *The Fearful Consequences of Ungodliness*

The repeated phrase *'God gave them up* (**1²⁴, ²⁶, ²⁸**) strikingly illustrates the Jewish tendency to insist on the sovereignty of God in His dealings with men. Today we more commonly think of 'secondary causes' and their 'consequences'. Where we should say that such and such things followed, Paul prefers to speak of the direct judgement of God.

1²⁴. *'in the lusts of their hearts'*, or, in modern speech, 'through the desires of their minds'.
'unto uncleanness', that is, impurity.
'that their bodies should be dishonoured'. The reference is to homosexuality. The phrase is explanatory: 'I mean the dishonouring . . .' See further **1²⁶⁻⁷**.

1²⁵⁻⁶. The worship and service due to God, Paul says, were given to man; truth was exchanged for a lie.
'for that they exchanged'. The Greek reads, 'Men who exchanged'.
The doxology *'who is blessed for ever. Amen'* is characteristically Jewish (cf. **9⁵**).
'vile passions'. Better, 'dishonourable passions' (*RSV*).

1²⁸. *'to have God in their knowledge'*. The translation is unduly literal. Read 'to recognize God'.

'*a reprobate mind*'. The phrase is variously rendered by commentators: Boylan uses the adjective 'worthless', the *RSV* has 'base'. What is implied is indicated by '*to do those things which are not fitting*', that is, morally fitting, seemly.

1[29-31]. These verses contain a terrible list of vices. The picture is overdrawn, for many virtues were esteemed in the pagan world, and Paul himself gives another side in 2[14-16].

'*covetousness*'. The Greek word can mean 'lust' (Moffatt). Dodd suggests 'ruthless self-assertion'.

'*malignity*'. So also Moffatt and the *RSV*. Sanday and Headlam say that it is 'the tendency to put the worst construction upon everything'.

'*backbiters*'. Better, 'slanderers'.

'*without natural affection*'. Or 'heartless' (*RSV*). Some MSS add '*implacable*'.

1[32]. '*but consent with them*'. The idea is that of applauding besides doing, which makes the condition worse.

(c) 2[1-16]: *The Judgement of God*

In this sub-section Paul appears to be thinking of wrong-doers in general, Gentiles and Jews alike. God, it is insisted, is no respecter of persons (2[12-16]). Sinful men are without excuse and judgement is certain, first upon Jews, in view of their advantages (cf. 3[2], 9[4-5]), but also upon Gentiles.

2[1-2]. '*without excuse*' (cf. 1[20]). The word used can mean 'without defence', 'with nothing to say'; and this meaning agrees better with the fact that in judging others, men judge themselves (cf. Matt 7[1]).

'*according to truth*', that is 'according to reality'.

2[3-4]. These verses break down man's defences, his easy conscience in judging others, his presumption in pleading God's goodness.

'*forbearance*' (cf. 3[25]).

'*leadeth thee to repentance*'. The Greek present tense here has the force of 'is intended to lead'. Paul rarely mentions repentance (cf. 2 Cor 7[9-10]). But, of course, the idea of a turning of mind and heart to God is frequently emphasized by him. Thus in 1 Thessalonians 1⁹ Paul says, 'ye turned unto God from idols, to serve a living and true God'.

2⁵⁻⁶. '*after*' here means 'in accordance with' or 'by'. The real situation is that the man is storing up wrath against himself. Paul is referring to the final judgement, as the quotation from Ps 62¹² suggests. For the moment he is thinking of God's action apart from His mercy in Christ.

2⁷⁻⁸. '*by patience in well-doing*', or 'patiently doing good' (Moffatt), in seeking glory, honour, and immortality.

'*eternal life*' is the reward; grammatically it is the object of the verb 'render' (understood). See verse **6**.

'*them that are factious*', that is, men who act from self-interest and obey unrighteousness, not truth.

'*shall be wrath and indignation*'. The rendering 'and fury' would be better. The words 'shall be' have to be understood because of a change in the construction, which otherwise would run, 'He will render . . .'.

2⁹. The verse continues the theme of **8*b***.

'*anguish*' well renders the Greek word which originally denoted painful pressure.

Verses 7–9 seem to teach a doctrine of works. But this cannot be Paul's meaning, since justification by faith is a dominating principle in the Epistle. For the moment he is considering, not what man can plead, but what God requires. He has yet to show that the works God rewards spring from faith.

2¹⁰⁻¹¹. This explanation applies also to the phrase '*worketh good*'. Paul has no use for a faith which is not expressed in works.

'*to the Jew first*', because of his privileges.

'*and also to the Greek*', because of natural revelation.

That God is without partiality is a basic principle of true religion. Cf. Col 3²⁵, Eph 6⁹, Jas 2¹.

2¹². '*without the law*' means without a knowledge of the Mosaic Law, the *Torah* (or teaching) given to the Jew. The Rabbis commented on the Law (in the *Mishnah*), and interpreted it in Aramaic paraphrases (the Babylonian and Jerusalem *Targums*) variously dated from the fourth to the seventh century A.D. In Paul's day oral tradition supplemented the Law (cf. Mark 7[11-13]).

'*shall also perish without the law*'. Judgement falls upon the Gentile because of what God has written in his heart; upon the Jew because the Law itself condemns him.

2[13]. '*just*'. Better 'righteous'.

'*shall be justified*'. The Greek verb 'to justify' means 'to declare righteous', not 'to make righteous'. This is the first time Paul has used this verb in *Romans*, and it is to be noted that he does not use it here with reference to Justification by faith, but simply to make the statement that it is not merely those who listen to the reading of the law who are pronounced '*just before God*', but those who actually fulfil its demands. His distinctive teaching on Justification is given in 3[21] and onwards.

For the contrast between '*hearers*' and '*doers*' see also Jas 1[22-3].

2[14]. '*by nature*' does not mean 'in their own power', but 'without a knowledge of the written Law'. Note Paul's play on the word 'law' in the statement that Gentiles who have no law '*are a law unto themselves*'.

2[15]. '*the law written in their hearts*', in contrast to the Mosaic Law. Cf. Jer 31[33], which speaks of a new covenant given to Israel, not, however, of 'natural revelation'.

'*conscience*'. The Stoics had made familiar to the ancient world the idea of an inner judgement which pronounces upon the character of men's actions. See also 9[1], 1 Cor 10[28-9], 2 Cor 1[12], 4[2], 5[11], and Heb 9[14]. The New Testament nowhere suggests that conscience is an instinctive knowledge of right and wrong in the mind of man. See further below.

2[16]. It has been conjectured that originally verse **16** followed **13**. See Moffatt. In any case, the thought is connected with verses **12-13**.

Among the themes suggested in 1[18]-2[16] are: The Wrath of God; The Divine Revelation in Nature; The Consequences of Sin; and Conscience.

It may be said that these topics are more suitable for theological addresses than for sermons. It is true that a sermon is not a lecture, but Biblical Theology is the preacher's bread without which hearers languish. His task is to prepare and offer it to the people, no easy undertaking and accomplished with many failures and mistakes. But, unless the history of preaching lies, there is a hunger for the Word. Men need to hear of God's judgements, His self-disclosure, the results of being self-centred, and the nature and meaning of the inner voice which condemns and therefore guides us. And these are the themes named above. Conscience is one of the most important of these themes. It is still necessary to insist that it is not an instinctive knowledge of good and evil implanted by God, for this belief has a wide currency. As illustrating this delusion Cromwell's views on the sack of Waterford may be mentioned. Also John Newton's confession that, during a voyage on a slave ship, he never had sweeter communion with God. People would not disagree as sharply as they do if this were a true account of conscience. Conscience is the sense of condemnation we all feel when our standards of moral behaviour are flouted, and the feeling of approval we have when we have done what we believe to be right. The standards are the important thing, and both in our individual lives and in political and social relationships they can grow morally and spiritually in strength and clarity. But is it not highly significant that the voice of conscience reacts immediately to these standards?

(2)   2¹⁷⁻³⁸: The Corresponding Failure of the Jews

(a)   2¹⁷⁻²⁴: *The Count against the Jews*

The Jew, Paul contends, relies upon the Law, glories in God, knows His will, and believes himself to be a guide and a teacher, and yet breaks the Law and brings God's name into disrepute among the Gentiles.

2¹⁷⁻¹⁸. The long series of conditional clauses beginning with the words '*If thou bearest the name of a Jew*' continues to the end of verse **20**.

'*resteth upon the law*', that is, leans and relies upon it.

'*approvest the things that are excellent*'. This is probably the best way of rendering a phrase which could also be translated, 'provest the things that differ' (*RSV*m). Cf. Phil 1¹⁰.

2¹⁹⁻²⁰. '*a guide of the blind*'. Cf. Matt 15¹⁴, 23¹⁶⁻²⁶.

'*a corrector*'. A good rendering in which the *RV* and the *RSV* agree. The word describes a schoolmaster who exercises discipline. Cf. Heb 12⁹.

C

2²¹. In this verse the apodosis, or main clause, in the long conditional sentence begins. It takes the form of rhetorical questions. The point is that the Jew does not put into practice his own teaching about stealing, adultery, and idolatry.

2²². '*abhorrest*'. A very strong word.

'*dost thou rob temples?*' Cf. Acts 19³⁷, which shows that the charge was not infrequently brought against Jews.

2²³⁻⁴. Several of the best commentators think verse **23** is a statement, not a question. This view agrees well with verse **24**, which is a free quotation of Is 52⁵. If **23** is read as a statement it is a definite accusation, 'You who make your boast in the law by your transgression of the law dishonour God'. So Barrett, p. 54. 'While you take pride in the law, you dishonour God by breaking it' (*NEB*).

(b) 2²⁵⁻⁹ : *Circumcision*

Circumcision was the sign of membership in the Jewish nation. Paul holds that it is of value only if the Law is obeyed. Obedience is the mark of the true Jew.

2²⁵. '*Thy circumcision is become uncircumcision*'. That is, it loses its meaning. In '*uncircumcision*' Paul is using a Jewish technical term. In verses **26-7** it is used to describe the Gentile.

2²⁶⁻⁷. The contention is that, when a Gentile keeps the Law, he is not inferior to the Jew. Indeed, he judges the Jew who, with the advantage of the written Law and circumcision, breaks the Law.

2²⁸⁻⁹. First negatively (**28**), and then positively (**29**), Paul defines the true Jew in spiritual, as opposed to purely physical, terms. In '*praise*' there is a play on words, for 'Judah' means 'praise'. Cf. Gen 29³⁵, 49⁸.

(c) 3¹⁻⁸ : *Objections Refuted*

In this section the Apostle answers objections which might be raised in view of what he has said.

3¹⁻². What is the Jew's privilege, and wherein lies the value of circumcision? The answer is '*Much every way*'. But, although Paul says 'First', he mentions one point only. The Jews '*were intrusted with the oracles of God*'. It was to them that He spoke.

3³⁻⁴. Again, is God's faithfulness annulled by the faithlessness of some Jews? Paul is thinking of the promises of God. The answer is 'By no means' ('*God forbid*'). 'Let God be true, though every man were false!', and Ps 51⁴ is quoted.

'*As it is written, That thou mightest be justified in thy words, and mightest prevail when thou comest into judgement*'. These are the words in Ps 51⁴ mentioned above. It is not easy at first sight to see why Paul introduces this quotation, but in fact he has good reason to do so.

The psalmist is thinking of a law-court in which God Himself is acquitted or declared to be in the right in the declaration that it was against Him alone that he had sinned. Paul may have been attracted to the quotation because of his interest in Justification, although at the moment he is not expounding that doctrine. As he uses it here he is thinking of the charge against God implied in the question, '*Shall their want of faith make of none effect the faithfulness of God?*' (verse 3), and by means of the quotation he argues that God is not open to this charge. As the psalmist had said, when judged, He is vindicated. The Jew loses his case.

'*justified*', that is, declared to be in the right. The quotation is important because it shows how Paul interpreted the verb. He anticipates what he is going to say about Justification in 3²¹⁻³¹. We have already noted a similar example in 2¹³.

3⁵⁻⁶. The third objection is: If man's sin commends God's righteousness, why then should he be condemned? For the moment all that Paul says is, '*then how shall God judge the world?*', a belief which he accepts as axiomatic.

3⁷⁻⁸. The objection is carried farther. Some had reported him to say: '*why not . . . . Let us do evil, that good may come?*' Why judge a man 'a sinner' when his act leads to God's glory? Paul's reply is terse: such men deserve condemnation! Clearly, as the parenthesis shows, his teaching about judgement and sin had exposed him to such objections.

It is remarkable that a section like 2^{17}-3^8 suggests subjects of very modern interest. These include: The Perils of Privilege; 'Rank is but the guinea's stamp'; Self-justification. Self-justification is the constant temptation of individuals and nations. Many examples can be found in history and literature.

(3) 3^{9-20}: The Universality of Sin

That all men, Jews and Gentiles alike, are sinners is a cardinal principle of the Apostle's theology. Like the Rabbis he bases this conviction upon the teaching of Scripture, but the later passage, 7^{7-25}, shows that he found it amply confirmed by human experience, his own and that of others.

3^9. *'are we in worse case than they?'* It is not clear whether by *'we'* Paul means Jews or Gentiles, and this difficulty is increased by the ambiguity of the Greek verb which he uses. The *RV*m reads, 'Do we excuse ourselves?'; the *AV*, 'Are we better than they?', and the *RSV*, 'Are we Jews any better off?' (cf. Moffatt). All these translations are possible. Fortunately, the general sense is clear. Presumably, Paul is speaking of the Jews, but in either case he says expressly **(9b)** that both Jews and Gentiles are 'under sin'.

'we before laid to the charge'. Or, more simply, 'have already charged'. The allusion is to 1^{18}-2^{29}.

'No, in no wise'. The Greek phrase can mean 'Not entirely' (cf. 1 Cor 5^{10}), but here means 'Certainly not'.

'under sin', that is, 'under the sway of sin'. Paul does not define sin, but he manifestly means spiritual slavery, resulting from disobedience to the mind and will of God. See notes on Chapters **6** and **7**.

3^{10-18}. The passages quoted include Ps 14^{1-3}, 5^9, 140^3, 10^7, Is 59^{7-8}, and Ps 36^1. The climax is reached in the last passage: *There is no fear of God before their eyes'*. Paul may have made this collection of Old Testament passages himself, but it is quite probable that it had already been compiled for purposes of instruction. It is increasingly recognized that candidates for baptism received instruction in Christian beliefs and that in this teaching lists of Old Testament passages were used. Cf. the phrase in 6^{17}, *'that form of teaching'*, also Mark 9^{42-50}.

3^{19}. '*them that are under the law*', that is, the Jews. But the universality of sin is emphatically expressed in the words '*every mouth*' and '*all the world*'.

'*brought under the judgement of God*'. More literally, 'become answerable to God'.

3^{20}. The verse states another basic Pauline principle: that no human being shall be justified in God's sight by the works of the Law.

'*the works of the law*', that is, the deeds it demands.

'*no flesh*'. Here used in the sense of 'no man'.

'*justified*', 'declared righteous', not 'made righteous'. See the note on 2^{13}. The reason given is that '*through the law cometh the knowledge of sin*', a truth which the Apostle intends to treat later (cf 7$^{7-8}$).

The outstanding theme of the section is the Universality of Sin, the realistic recognition of which is the background of the Christian message set out in the vital passage (3$^{21-31}$) which follows. No greater affront to human pride can be given than this teaching, provided sin is seen as a state of mind toward God, and not simply as a breach of an ethical code. Sin needs to be distinguished from sins such as stealing, murder, adultery, false witness, and the like. A man may have committed none of these acts and yet for all that be a sinner, or as Paul puts it, be '*under sin*'. The essence of sin is self-interest, self-rule. See the Glossary. The older preachers made dramatic use of the Old Testament stories of Cain, Samson, and David, and there is much to be said still for this method, but the modern preacher has also examples taken from the life of today, and what is more in the attitudes of communities and nations. Living to oneself is the cause of human ills and is so subtle in its onset that it may not be perceived under the disguise of respectability. In *The Idea of Perfection* R. N. Flew effectively quotes the words of James Martineau, 'Moral evil is the only thing in creation of which it is decreed that the more we are familiar with it, the less we know of it.' 'Our worst sins', writes Dr Flew (p. 333), 'are often those of which we are unconscious.' In the mercy of God, however, depravity is not total. There is a prevenient grace of God in the work of the Holy Spirit in the hearts of all men. This is a great and a timely theme.

(4) 3$^{21-31}$: The New Righteousness; Justification by Faith

This part of the Epistle takes up the note first struck in 1^{17}. It sets forth the righteous activity of God in Christ. It is not satisfactory to describe 1^{18}-3^{20} as a parenthesis. It is the foundation upon which what is now to be said stands. Man as a sinner is the pre-supposition of the saving work of God. This work Paul now describes.

3^{21}. '*But now apart from the law a righteousness of God hath been manifested, being witnessed by the law and the prophets*'. '*But now*', that is, in the present time.

'*apart from the law*'. Alternatively to it, and in contrast with it.

'*a righteousness of God*'. See the note on 1^{17}.

'*being witnessed*'. This is maintained in 3^{31} and 4^{1-25}. Paul attaches the greatest importance to the fact that the saving activity of God is foreshadowed in the law and the prophets.

3^{22}. '*through faith in Jesus Christ*' explains how the righteousness is apprehended, namely, by dependence upon Christ. This is further brought out in the words, '*unto all them that believe*', and '*all*' is underlined by the words, '*there is no distinction*'.

3^{23}. '*all have sinned*'. '*The glory of God*', of which men '*fall short*', is the divine image in which he was created. Cf. 1 Cor 11^7.

3^{24}. '*being justified freely by his grace*'. The phrase links on to verse 22. Man is declared righteous apart from anything he can do. All springs from the spontaneous, unmerited love of God.

'*through the redemption*', that is, the deliverance effected by Christ. Cf. Mark 10^{45}. Paul may well be thinking of the act of manumission by which a slave was set free. Manumission is described by A. Deissmann in his *Light from the Ancient East*, p. 322. In this ancient rite the owner brings the slave to the heathen temple and sells him to the god, receiving money which the slave has paid to the temple treasury. 'The slave is now the property of the god; not, however, a slave of the temple, but a protégé of the god. Against all the world, especially his former master, he is a completely free man.' But Paul may also have in mind the Deliverance of Israel from Egypt.

3²⁵⁻⁶. *'Whom God set forth to be a propitiation, through faith, by his blood, to shew his righteousness, because of the passing over of the sins done aforetime, in the forbearance of God; For the shewing, I say, of his righteousness at this present season: that he might himself be just, and the justifier of him that hath faith in Jesus'.* This is a passage of outstanding importance in Paul's teaching.

'*set forth*', that is, 'set forth publicly, for all to see', upon the Cross.

'*to be a propitiation*'. The word '*propitiation*' is so much associated with the pagan idea of appeasing God that it is misleading. The word 'expiation' is better, if by this we mean the act of covering or making atonement for sin. Many commentators translate the Greek word (*hilasterion*) by 'Mercy-seat', as in Heb 9⁵, since it was used in the Greek Bible to denote the lid or covering of the ark (Ex 25¹⁷) on which blood was sprinkled on the Day of Atonement. More probably the word is an adjective, describing the sense in which Christ was '*set forth*', namely, 'as a means of atonement' making God and man 'at one'. Some commentators take the word to be a neuter noun meaning 'an expiatory sacrifice', or 'an expiatory person'. *NEB*, 'the means of expiating sin'.

'*by his blood*', that is, by His outpoured life given in sacrifice. The phrase is to be taken with '*set forth*'. Barrett, pp. 75-82, translates 'This Christ Jesus God publicly set forth in his bloody sacrificial death as his means of dealing with sin, received through faith'.

'*through faith*', not 'faith in his blood' (*AV* and *RSV*m). The phrase describes the way in which Christ's Sacrifice is appropriated.

'*to shew his righteousness*', that is, to demonstrate it. The reason given is that in the past God might seem to have passed over sins in His forbearance (cf. 2⁴). Cf. Acts 17³⁰, 'The times of ignorance therefore God overlooked'.

This idea is repeated in verse **26,** with an emphasis on '*this present season*', and a further emphasis is laid on faith in the words '*him that hath faith in Jesus*'. In Christ God is shown both to be '*righteous*' in Himself and at the same time '*the justifier*' of the believing man.

3²⁷. The consequence is drawn that there is no room for human claims. All boasting is '*excluded*'.

'*law*' in this verse has the meaning of 'system'. Of this system the essence is faith, not works.

3²⁸. '*We reckon therefore that a man is justified by faith, apart from the works of the law*'. Here the truth of Justification by Faith is explicitly stated.

3²⁹⁻³⁰. A further argument is based on monotheism.

'*if so be that God is one*' is best attached, after a comma, to the preceding verse. Doubt is not suggested, but certainty ('If indeed').

No sharp distinction is to be drawn between '*by faith*' and '*through faith*'. The antithesis is rhetorical. The point is that faith is essential to all, to Jew and Gentile alike.

3³¹. '*the law*' here means the *Torah*. (See **2¹²**.) So far from destroying it, his teaching, Paul claims, establishes it, that is, its deepest principles.

The main theme of the section is manifestly Justification by Faith. In expounding this doctrine today it is essential to insist that it is God's way of putting men right with Himself, that it is an act of God's grace and not man's effort, that it is accomplished by Christ's Sacrifice and received by faith alone. It is not a fiction, since the new relationship is the source and first step in the way of righteousness, expressed in, but not merited by, works. Utter dependence is the beginning of the Christian life. Men still try to win God's favour. It is the preacher's responsibility to insist that it can only be received when the last cry of pride is stilled. But it must also be pointed out that Justification is only a beginning, to be followed by growth in Perfect Love, that is, in Sanctification. In thinking of Justification the main points to be noted are (1) that it is initiated by God, (2) that it deals with a man in his immediate condition, (3) that it is conditioned by faith, and (4) that its basis is Christ's atoning work. See further the full discussion in my book, *Forgiveness and Reconciliation* (pp. 29-69). Luther described the doctrine as 'the article by which a Church stands or falls'.

(5) 4¹⁻²⁵: The Example of Abraham's Faith

This section discusses the character of Abraham's faith in its bearings on the teaching set forth in **3²¹⁻³¹**. But it does more; it shows the necessary connexion between the new way of redemption in Christ and the Old Testament promises.

4¹. *'our forefather'* is the language of a supposed Jewish objector. It also suggests that Abraham is the father of all who believe, as explained in verses **11-12.**

'according to the flesh', that is, by human descent (cf. **1³**).

'hath found' should probably be omitted on textual grounds; cf. *RV*m and *RSV*. In this case the passage runs, 'What then shall we say of Abraham, our forefather according to the flesh?'

4². This verse continues the objection. Justified by works, Abraham has something to boast about! Paul's brief comment is *'but not toward God'*.

4³⁻⁵. The reply is expanded. First, Gen 15⁶ is quoted in the form, *'Abraham believed God, and it was reckoned unto him for righteousness'*. The reference is to God's promise that his seed should be as the stars. Secondly, Paul points out that the reward of one who works is a matter of debt, not of grace, but for one who believes the reverse is true: *'his faith is reckoned for righteousness'*.

'him that justifieth the ungodly'. The context and the word *'reckoned'* clearly show that 'to justify' is to *deem* or *declare* righteous (cf. **2¹³**), and *'ungodly'* excludes any claim to merit.

4⁶⁻⁷. Further support is drawn from Ps 32¹⁻², in which the Psalmist pronounces blessed the man *'to whom the Lord will not reckon sin'*.

4⁸⁻¹⁰. Taking up the word *'blessing'* (verse **6**), Paul asks if it applies to Abraham when he was circumcised, or when he was yet uncircumcised, and relying on Gen 17¹⁰⁻¹¹, which of course follows Gen 15⁶, he argues that righteousness was reckoned to him *before* he was circumcised.

4¹¹⁻¹². Circumcision is described in Gen 17¹¹ as *'a token of a covenant betwixt me and you'*, and Paul maintains that it was *'a seal of the righteousness of the faith which he had while he was in uncircumcision'*. Thus Abraham is the father of circumcised and uncircumcised alike, since everything depends on faith. The modern reader justly finds a certain artificiality in the argument, which is Rabbinical in character, but the main point is clear that circumcision had nothing to do with the fact that Abraham's faith was counted for righteousness.

4¹³⁻¹⁴. Paul now takes up the promise made to Abraham that he should be *'heir of the world'* (cf. Gen 18¹⁸, 22¹⁷⁻¹⁸), and maintains that it was not based on any legal principle (*'not through the law'*), but *'through the righteousness of faith'*. Were it otherwise, faith would be null and the promise void.

4¹⁵. Parenthetically, he observes that the Law brings wrath and transgression. These points are treated later in 7¹⁰⁻²⁵.

4¹⁶⁻¹⁷. These verses are difficult because Paul writes under deep feeling and leaves something to be supplied by the reader.

'for this cause it is of faith'. *'It'* is left unexplained, but is either *'the promise'* (verses **13-14**) or the inheritance (suggested by the word *'heirs'* in verse **14**). The same ambiguity appears in *'that it may be according to grace'*. Faith, it is claimed, is essential because everything depends on grace, the unmerited love of God. The end in view is that the divine promise may be guaranteed to all Abraham's seed, physical and spiritual alike.

That Abraham is *'the father of us all'* is supported by quoting Gen 17⁵.

'before him whom he believed, even God'. The construction of the sentence is loose, but the idea is that Abraham receives the promise in God's presence that he is to be the father of many nations. See Gen 17¹⁻⁴.

'quickeneth the dead', or 'makes alive the dead'.

'calleth', or 'summons'. God calls into being *'the things that are not, as though they were'*.

The reference is to the birth of Isaac (verses **18-21**).

4¹⁸⁻¹⁹. *'who in hope believed against hope'*. A striking characterization of Abraham's faith in God's promise!

'he considered'. Some MSS insert 'not' (*AV*). But the point of the statement is that he did consider facts, and yet believed.

4²⁰⁻². *'he wavered not through unbelief'*. For the verb see 14²³, also Mark 11²³ and Jas 1⁶. On the contrary, by his faith he became strong, giving glory to God. The point is pressed home that it was this full confidence of his in God's power to fulfil His promise which was counted to Abraham for righteousness.

4²³⁻⁴. The claim that Gen 15⁶ was written *'for our sake also'* is forceful so far as the quality of Abraham's faith is concerned, but is artificial if pressed farther, for there is an essential difference between his faith and justifying faith. Abraham's faith is fidelity in respect of a divine promise; the Christian believer's faith is personal dependence upon Christ and is not only trust in God who raised Him from the dead.

'Jesus our Lord' is the primitive Christian confession. Cf. 10⁹. See the note on 1⁴.

4²⁵. *'who was delivered up for our trespasses'*. This is a statement, probably taken over by Paul, which reflects primitive Christian belief shaped by the idea of the Suffering Servant of the Lord in Is 53. To it the Apostle adds a clause which brings in the idea of justification and so connects the whole with his main argument.

'and was raised for our justification'. Despite a similar antithesis in 5¹⁰, it is mistaken exegesis to separate the two clauses too sharply, as if the death is to be connected with forgiveness, but the resurrection with justification. As a matter of fact 5⁹ connects justification with Christ's blood. The clauses must be taken together. Christ died and rose again for our trespasses and our justification.

'for', in both clauses, probably means 'because of', but in the second clause some commentators take it to mean 'with a view to'. On grammatical grounds it is doubtful if this rendering of the Greek proposition can be sustained, and it is better to translate both phrases alike, 'because of our trespasses' and 'because of our justification'. See *Exp. T*, vol. L, p. 298 (V. Taylor), p. 564 (H. G. Meecham).

The main theme of the section is Abraham's faith. The two passages, *'Who in hope believed against hope'*, and, *'He wavered not through unbelief'*, stand out. But in the main the chief interest of the section is theological. So far as Justification is concerned, the preacher of today will feel that, for all the suggestiveness of Paul's illustration from the Old Testament, a better approach to the doctrine is made by the teaching of Jesus in the Parable of the Lost Son (Luke 15¹¹⁻³²). In his interesting and important book, *The Parables of Jesus*, J. Jeremias writes, 'The parable describes with touching simplicity what God is like, his goodness, his grace, his boundless mercy, his abounding love. He rejoices over the return of the lost, like the father who prepared the feast of welcome' (p. 105). The second part (relating to the elder brother), he suggests, is addressed to men who were offended at the gospel. The parable contains, in the setting of family relationships, the same ideas which Paul treats in legal language.

(6) 5^1-11^: The Results of Justification

These are peace with God, hope and joy.

5^1^. *'let us have peace with God'*. While this is the most strongly attested reading, it is probable that Paul wrote, 'We have peace with God' (*AV* and *RSV*). The difference in the Greek is simply that between a long and a short letter 'o', which were often confused in pronunciation. Similarly 'we rejoice' is to be preferred in verse **2.**

'peace with God' (cf. Eph 2^14-17^, Col 1^20^) is the peace of complete reconciliation with Him. Cf. 5^10f^.

5^2^. This peace with God is further described as *'this grace wherein we stand'*, a condition made possible by God's free unmerited love.

'access', or 'introduction' or 'approach'. Outside the New Testament the word is used of a landing-stage.

'by faith' describes the means by which we obtain peace. The whole passage sounds a note of exultation (cf. 8^31-39^)

The *'hope of the glory of God'* belongs to the consummation of God's purposes, and so is eschatological, but it is also enjoyed already here and now.

5^3-4^. *'let us rejoice'*. Again 'We rejoice' is better. See the note on verse **1.**

The rejoicing even embraces *'tribulations'* in the knowledge that these yield endurance (a better rendering than *'patience'*), endurance yields *'probation'* (or 'approvedness'), and this in turn *'hope'*.

5^5^. This hope does not prove illusory (*'putteth not to shame'*) for a very good reason; *'the love of God'* (that is, God's love for us) has been poured into our hearts through the Holy Spirit which was given to us. The Spirit is the medium of the love. What is involved is brought out in verses **6-8.**

5⁶⁻⁸. '*Christ died for the ungodly*'. This startling fact is the more marvellous because it happened '*while we were yet weak*', that is, incapable, and '*in due season*', at the right time in the counsels of God. Cf. Gal 4⁴, 2 Cor 6², Eph 1¹⁰. More astonishing than sacrifice for '*a righteous man*', or even '*a good man*', is the fact that this death was on behalf of sinners ('*while we were yet sinners*'). The statement that '*God commendeth his own love toward us*' completely rules out any doctrine of the Cross which sets God and Christ over against each other. It was out of the experimental basis described in verses **5-8** that the doctrine of the Trinity came to be formulated. The passage mentions the love of God, its shedding abroad in our hearts by the Holy Spirit, and the work of Christ in dying for the ungodly. See also **8²⁻³**.

5⁹. '*Much more then*'. A still fuller mercy is described. Justified now, we shall be saved from condemnation at the last. The constant interweaving of present with eschatological salvation is a marked feature in Paul's teaching.

'*justified by his blood*'. See the note on **3²⁵**. This passage directly bases justification upon Christ's Sacrifice.

'*the wrath*' (here without '*of God*'). See **1¹⁸, 3⁵, 9²²**.

5¹⁰⁻¹¹. These verses give the reason for belief in final salvation.

'*while we were enemies*' is parallel to '*while we were yet sinners*' (verse **8**), and '*we were reconciled to God*' is another way of saying '*we have peace with God*' (verse **1**) in consequence of justification.

Reconciliation is the restoration of sinful men to fellowship with God. Cf. 2 Cor 5¹⁸⁻²⁰, Eph 2¹⁶, Col 1¹⁹⁻²². It is an act of God through Christ rather than a process. The process in Paul's thought is salvation, and it is consummated at the Last Judgement. We shall understand these distinctions best if we remember that in Jewish teaching God declares men righteous or otherwise at the last, and that Paul brings Justification into the present by his doctrine of faith in Christ. His eschatology is 'realized'. But he does not renounce the idea of final judgement (cf. **14¹⁰**, 2 Cor 5¹⁰) any more than Jesus did.

For 'realized eschatology' see C. H. Dodd, *The Parables of the Kingdom*, pp. 34-51. Dr Dodd defines it as 'the impact upon this world of the "powers of the world to come" in a series of events, unprecedented and unrepeatable, now in actual progress'. See also Dodd, *Romans*, pp. 51-61.

'*by his life*', that is, through fellowship with Christ and in view of His priestly ministry on high (8³⁴).

'*not only so*'. Paul returns to his emphasis upon joy and the fact that '*we have now received the reconciliation*' through our Lord Jesus Christ.

In this short section of eleven verses the main themes of Pauline teaching are gathered and combined—justification, peace with God, the love of God poured into the heart by the Holy Spirit, the proof of God's love in the death of Christ, salvation, judgement, sanctification, and reconciliation. Each is a preacher's theme, as timely today as when Paul first wrote. Each can become a revelation to the most sophisticated congregation. It is a tragedy to neglect them and a crime to make them dull. They shine in their own light when the lantern is clear. In particular the passage 5⁸, '*God commendeth his own love toward us, in that, while we were yet sinners, Christ died*' states what is the very heart of the gospel. But along with this emphasis upon what Christ has done for us we need to insist, as Paul does, upon His present and future work, '*Much more, being reconciled, shall we be saved by his life*'.

(7) 5¹²⁻²¹: Christ as the Second Adam

Having assigned a decisive place to Christ's death in relation to man's standing with God, Paul now goes on to discuss His relation to mankind, as the Head of a new humanity. It is for this reason that he contrasts Christ with Adam.

Little is said of the Fall in the Old Testament, but a connexion between Adam's sin and the wickedness of his descendants is suggested in Gen 6⁵, ¹¹⁻¹². In the Apocrypha the connexion between his sin and death is affirmed (cf. Wisdom 2²³⁻⁴, Ecclesiasticus 25²⁴, 4 Ezra (2 Esdras) 3⁷, ²¹⁻²), but with an emphasis upon man's responsibility (cf. 4 Ezra 8⁵⁹⁻⁶⁰, 9¹¹). In Paul's day Jewish teachers held the same view, and so also in later times.

Paul's teaching reflects contemporary ideas at a point before they were hardened into the doctrine of Original Sin. The Apostle does not teach that men share in Adam's guilt, but sees the consequences of his trespass in the powers of sin and death which hold men in thraldom. We have less confidence today in believing in the existence of a historical Adam, but there can be no doubt of the reality of the bondage which Paul describes in terms of this mythology and of man's inability to set himself free. Deep down in 'the unconscious' there is a legacy of evil which comes to us from the past and from our social environment which can only be overcome by the grace of God.

The main interest of the section is not Adam or Original Sin, but Christ as the Second Adam, the founder and head of a new humanity. This teaching stands in its own right, apart from what is said, or may be said, of Adam.

5¹². '*as through one man*', that is, through Adam, who is thought of as the head of fallen mankind.

'*sin entered into the world*'. Here Sin is personified as a demonic power (cf. **6¹², ¹⁴**) with Death in its train.

'*and so death passed unto all men*'. Death also is presented as a tyrant.

'*for that all sinned*'. The conjunction '*for*' is vague. The Greek is better rendered 'because' or 'inasmuch as'. The clause gives the reason why Death's sway became universal. A direct connexion with Adam's transgression is not explicitly asserted, but it cannot be Paul's meaning that men sinned independently of their ancestors. A racial situation is described. Like the Rabbis, Paul wishes to preserve man's responsibility, while describing a racial heritage.

The sentence is not completed. Perhaps Paul meant to add: 'So through one man [Christ] righteousness came into the world, and life through righteousness.' His attention is diverted to the points raised in verses **13-14.**

5¹³⁻¹⁴. Sin was in the world, Paul declares, before the Law was given, '*but sin*', he says, '*is not imputed when there is no law*'.

'*not imputed*', that is, not set down to one's account. The difficulty then arises: Why, in this case, the penalty of death? Perhaps Paul intends us to recall his previous teaching about the law written in the heart (**2¹²⁻¹⁵**). The existence of this 'law', to the extent that it includes a knowledge of right and wrong, is the measure of man's responsibility.

'*Nevertheless death reigned*'. Manifestly, more than physical death is meant. A power holding men in thrall is pictured.

'*who is a figure of him that was to come*'. Adam, it is suggested, is a type of Christ.

5¹⁵. Paul holds that the reality transcends the type in every respect. Over against '*the trespass*' stands '*the free gift*'; in contrast with death is '*the grace of God*'.

'*the one*' is Adam.

'*the many*'. The phrase does not mean 'some', but by a common Semitic idiom (cf Mark 10[45]) distinguishes 'all' from the one. In our idiom therefore '*the many*' = 'all men'.

'*by the grace*'. The Greek phrase, which lacks the definite article, probably qualifies '*the free gift*', 'the free gift by grace'. This '*gift*', Paul says, is imparted by Jesus Christ and it abounds '*unto the many*', that is, as explained above, to all men. 'The many' in both cases has same meaning.

5[16]. Further the effects are different. '*The judgement*' brought '*condemnation*'; '*the free gift*' brings '*justification*' in the sense of 'acquittal'. See below.

'*came . . . came*'. The verbs are wanting in the Greek and have to be supplied from the context.

'*of one . . . of many trespasses*'. Probably '*from* one . . . *from* many trespasses' is better.

'*justification*'. But the word used means 'a decree' or 'a sentence of acquittal', and this rendering suits the context. The word is legal, but the action is one of grace.

5[17]. Still more is claimed. Over against the enthronement of Death stands the assurance that those who receive '*the abundance of grace and of the gift of righteousness*' shall '*reign in life*' through Jesus Christ. God's grace prevails over man's sin. This victory is followed by coronation, death by life.

5[18-19]. These verses recapitulate the argument almost in note form.

'*the judgement came . . . the free gift came*'. As the italics in the *RV* show, these words have to be understood from the context, as in verse **16**. The verbs 'issued' and 'issues' have been suggested (cf. Moffatt).

'*through one act of righteousness*'. So many commentators. But the word used is the same as in verse **16**, 'sentence of acquittal', and, I think, should be so rendered here. We ought not to allow ourselves to be repelled by the forensic language. It describes an act of divine grace.

'*justification of life*'. This phrase means justification which leads to life, life-giving justification. It states the result of the acquittal, a right standing with God which brings life.

'*disobedience*' and '*obedience*' state the contrast in another way, in spiritual instead of legal terms.

'*the many*'. See note on verse **15**.

'*were made sinners . . . be made righteous*'. The verb used means 'constituted', 'put into a certain category'. No one can be made a sinner or made righteous.

5$^{20-1}$. '*the law came in beside*'. The verb describes a stealthy entry. Cf. Gal 2^4.

'*that the trespass might abound*'. Some grammarians think that *result*, rather than *purpose*, is described. See 7$^{7-10}$.

'*grace did abound more exceedingly*'. A reign through righteousness leading to '*eternal life*' replaces the reign of sin 'over a charnel-house' (Sanday and Headlam); and this comes to be, says Paul, '*through Jesus Christ our Lord*'.

'*eternal life*', that is, life in all its fulness, the emphasis being on its quality more than its duration.

A preacher may well wonder how he can convey to others the note of exultation which pervades this difficult section. The main theme, Christ as the Head of a redeemed world, is surely timely in days when Sin and Death still stalk through the earth. Other great themes are the Kingdoms of Death and Life, the Gift of Eternal Life (cf. also 6^{23}), and, as in so many chapters in the Epistle, Grace Triumphant. Perhaps the most suggestive passage in the section is the second part of **5**^{20}, '*But where sin abounded, grace did abound more exceedingly*', which recognizes facts in declaring that sin abounded, as it does still, but claims that grace, the free unmerited love of God, abounded to a pre-eminent degree.

(8) 6$^{1-23}$: Dying to Sin through Union with Christ

In two sections (6$^{1-14}$ and 6$^{15-23}$) objections to the teaching about grace are considered, but the main purpose is positive. It affirms that, through union with Christ, the power of sin is broken and man is made free. '*Sin*', Paul declares, '*shall not have dominion over you*'.

6$^{1-2}$. The question, '*Shall we continue in sin, that grace may abound?*', is answered with an indignant negative. It is unthinkable!

'*We who died to sin*', or with an emphasis on quality, 'Men who died . . . how shall we . . . ?'

D

To die to sin is to be freed from its power, not necessarily to be sinless.

6³. An appeal is made to Baptism, which in primitive Christianity was by immersion.

'*baptized into Christ Jesus*' means to be made incorporate with Him, to become one with Him in the fellowship of the community.

'*baptized into his death*'. His death was His victory over sin, and to be baptized into His death is to share in His victory. That, says Paul in effect, is what your Baptism meant.

6⁴. The solemn act of immersion is a symbolic parallel to the death, burial, and resurrection of Christ, but Paul is far from describing Baptism as a mere symbolic action. A real experience of death to sin is suggested by '*baptism into death*'. The reference to resurrection emphasizes the positive side, '*newness of life*', that is emergence into a new way of life.

'*through the glory of the Father*' means by the splendour of His power.

6⁵⁻⁶. '*united*'. The word is used of the growth of plants and trees. A vital act of incorporation with Christ is therefore suggested. The Greek means 'united with', and '*him*' (as in *RV*) or 'his death' must be understood.

'*our old man*', 'our old self'.

'*crucified with him*'. Cf. Gal 2²⁰, 5²⁴, 6¹⁴.

'*the body of sin*'. See the Glossary. '*Body*' is here the sinful self, the self we see dominated by sin.

'*done away*', that is, 'destroyed'.

6⁷. '*For he that hath died is justified from sin*'. Here the meaning is legally free. 'Sin loses its suit' (Sanday and Headlam). The meaning is that the man who has died with Christ, through union with Him, is freed from the tyrant Sin. He is not sinless, for there are battles still to be fought, but he is no longer the slave of sin. He has been acquitted, set free. Nygren, *Romans*, p. 242, writes, 'That the Christian is "free from sin" means to Paul that by Christ sin is cast down from its throne'.

6⁸⁻⁹. Death with Christ means also life with Him. Special reference is made to Christ's risen life, in the power of which we share.

6$^{10-11}$. '*he died unto sin*', that is, in respect of it, in relation to it. Cf. verses **2** and **11**. A decisive victory on the part of Christ is meant.

'*once*'. Better 'once for all'. Cf. Heb 7^{27}, etc.

'*he liveth unto God*'. A continuous relationship is implied, The readers are to think of themselves in the same way, as dead to sin, but alive to God.

'*in Christ Jesus*'. This phrase is a summary description of union with Christ, a vital element in Paul's theology. Cf. 8^1, 1 Cor 1^{30}, 2 Cor 5^{17}, Phil 4$^{1, 13}$, 1 Thess 1^1, 3^8, and, with reference to the Holy Spirit, 14^7, 1 Cor 12^3.

6$^{12-13}$. The exhortation in this verse shows that Paul has in mind, not sinlessness, but freedom from the tyranny of Sin.

'*reign*'. Cf. verse **14** (of Death).

'*neither present your members*'. The Greek tense denotes continuous action, constant yielding.

'*but present yourselves unto God*'. Here, in contrast, a decisive act is implied.

'*yourselves*' and '*your members*' are not to be separated too sharply. Even the '*mortal body*' is not thought of as wholly physical, for in biblical teaching the person and the body are closely related and sometimes almost identified (cf. **12^1**).

'*instruments*'. The word used can mean 'weapons' (*RV*m). The figure is military. We are to be God's weapons.

6^{14}. The triumphant promise, '*Sin shall not have dominion over you*', makes it clear that all the way through this section freedom from a usurper is the basic idea. '*not under law, but under grace*' succinctly describes the new conditions under which the believer lives.

6$^{15-16}$. A new approach is made to the question, '*shall we sin?*', by the submission that we are the slaves of the master we obey.

Cf. Matt 6^{24}; '*No man can serve two masters.*'

'*servants*'. Better 'bondservants' (*RV*m), or 'slaves' (*RSV*).

6$^{17-18}$. Formerly '*slaves of sin*' (*RSV*), the readers were now '*slaves of righteousness*' (*RSV*).

'*from the heart*' denotes the radical character of the change.

'that form of teaching whereunto ye were delivered'. The phrase refers to the instruction concerning the new way of life given in connexion with Baptism.

6¹⁹. With an apology to his readers (cf. Gal 3¹⁵), Paul speaks more explicitly.

'because of the infirmity of your flesh' refers to their weak intellectual discernment.

'present' again implies a decisive act.

Over against their service to *'uncleanness'* and *'iniquity'* is set the exhortation to yield their members as the service of righteousness leading to sanctification.

'to iniquity unto iniquity' suggests one stage after another, but *'unto iniquity'* (omitted by some MSS) may be a later addition inserted to correspond to *'unto sanctification'*.

'sanctification' is the process of ever-increasing consecration to the worship and service of God. Its fulness is perfect love.

6²⁰⁻². In these verses there is a play on the word *'free'*. A delusive freedom, it is claimed, is replaced by one that is real.

The question mark in verse **21** should perhaps be placed earlier, *'What fruit then had ye at that time?'*, the answer being *'in the things whereof ye are now ashamed'*. Their end is described as *'death'*.

'being made free from sin' (as in verse **18**) is emancipation, not perfection, and on the positive side is balanced by the idea of service to God in the striking phrase, *'and have become slaves of God'* (RSV). This 'slavery' leads to *'sanctification'*, and its goal is *'eternal life'*. See verse **19** and **5²¹**.

6²³. *'For the wages of sin is death; but the free gift of God is eternal life in Christ Jesus our Lord'*. Sin, Paul declares, pays *'wages'* in the currency of *'death'*, while God's *'free gift'* is *'eternal life'*.

'wages'. The Greek word is used of 'rations' or 'soldiers' pay', and then generally of 'wages'. Cf. Luke 3¹⁴, 1 Cor 9⁷, 2 Cor 11⁸.

'eternal life'. See **5²¹**.

'in Christ Jesus our Lord', that is, in union with Him. Cf. 8³⁹. Compare also *'through Jesus Christ our Lord'* in **5²¹** and **7²⁵**.

The leading themes of the section are: Death to Sin, Union with Christ, Service which is Perfect Freedom, and Eternal Life. Each is a doctrine of personal Christian experience, but each, as Paul presents them, is bound up with the life of a believing community as the references to baptism, union with Christ, teaching, sanctification, and eternal life imply. We die to sin, live with Christ, learn, are consecrated, and find fullness of life in the fellowship of the Church which is the Body of Christ. It is to a community that he writes, and it is within that community that he looks to see the individual freed, nourished, and perfected. For the preacher the two texts which stand out in this section are 6[14], '*For sin shall not have dominion over you: for ye are not under the law, but under grace*', and 6[23], '*For the wages of sin is death; but the free gift of God is eternal life in Christ Jesus our Lord*'. In treating these texts exposition is essential; in the first 'sin', 'law', and 'grace' all need to be explained in modern terms, and in the second 'death' and 'eternal life'.

(9) 7[12-25]: Freedom from Legal Bondage

While the Mosaic Law is in mind throughout this section of the Epistle, the wider question of legal righteousness is the dominating issue. First, freedom from the bondage of law is treated (6[1-6]), and secondly, the vanity of legal righteousness (7[7-25]).

(a) 7[1-6]: Freedom from the Bondage of Law

7[1]. '*are ye ignorant?*' has the force of 'Surely you know', as 6[3].

'*men that know the law*', or better '*law*' (*RV*m), that is law in general.

The point made is that the dominion of law ends with death.

7[2-3]. This principle is illustrated by the case of marriage, which is terminated by death.

'*the law of the husband*', that is the law relating to the husband.

'*an adulteress*'. Cf. the sayings of Jesus in Matt 5[32], Mark 10[11-12], and Luke 16[18].

Paul is not discussing the questions of marriage and divorce (cf. 1 Cor 7), but only a single legal fact, that with the death of the first husband the wife is free.

7⁴. The illustration is only partially successful, for, in **7¹⁴⁻²⁵**
it is not the law that dies, but the believer who dies to the law.

'*Through the body of Christ*'. This difficult phrase refers
to the crucified person of Christ, and to the experience of
dying with Him (cf. **6⁶**) rather than, as some think, to the
Church (cf. **12⁵**, 1 Cor 12²⁷), especially since '*another*' is identified as the Risen Christ.

C. H. Dodd reminds us that for Paul, the Body of Christ is
the Church (1 Cor 12²⁷, Eph 1²³, &c.). He suggests that he
took this idea so seriously, as embodying 'the corporate personality' of Christ, that in the death of Christ on the cross
'he always saw the death of the whole people of God to sin,
law, and the flesh', *Romans*, p. 102. But the phrase 'the body
of Christ' is not used in *Romans* of the Church, though the
simile '*one body in Christ*' is used in **12⁵**.

The word '*joined*' and the reference to '*fruit*' show that
union with Christ is here conceived under the figure of marriage.

7⁵⁻⁶. These verses set past and present in contrast. Formerly,
Paul says, '*we were in the flesh*', and '*sinful passions*', stimulated
by the law, worked in us ('*in our members*'), so as to produce
fruits in the service of death. Now, on the contrary, our dying
with Christ has set us free from the law. We are now the
slaves of God in a new way of life directed by the Spirit, not
in the old manner of living regulated by a written code.

'*in the flesh*', that is, in our self-centred humanity.

'*sinful passions*' are feelings and emotions leading to sin.

'*which were through the law*'. This stimulating effect of the
law is treated later in verses **9-11**.

'*in newness of the spirit*'. The phrase anticipates the teaching
concerning the Holy Spirit in Chapter **8**.

'*not in oldness of the letter*' is a summary description of life
lived in obedience to written law.

(b) **7⁷⁻²⁵** :   *The Vanity of Legal Righteousness*

There can be little doubt that this section reflects Paul's own experience as he looks back upon it from the standpoint of his Christian
outlook. In the history of interpretation opinion has been, and
still is, much divided upon the question whether it describes his
pre-conversion experience or his spiritual condition at the time of

writing. If we have to choose between these two alternatives, the former seems the more probable, but either view has its difficulties. It seems likely therefore that, while Paul is describing his experience before he saw Christ on the Damascus road, he also pictures the state of impotence of any one who relies upon himself at any time in his endeavour to meet the claims of a legal code of righteousness

7⁷⁻⁸. Sharply denying that the law is sin, Paul says that he would not have known sin had it not been for the law. He illustrates this fact by the commandment, '*Thou shalt not covet*', apart from which, he says, he would not have known what coveting is.

Sin grasped the opportunity provided by the command and led him to all kinds of coveting. Again, in this account, Sin is half personified.

'*finding occasion*'. The word used has a military meaning. It denotes 'a base of operations', 'a place to start'.

'*for apart from the law sin is dead*'. Cf. 3²⁰, 4¹⁵, 5³⁰. There is perhaps a certain amount of overstatement in the passage (cf. 2¹⁴⁻¹⁵), but the main point is clear. A prohibition arouses desire, and so creates the consciousness of sin.

7⁹⁻¹¹. '*I was alive apart from the law once*'. Paul is recalling a happy innocent childhood.

'*Sin revived*'. Better 'sprang to life' (T. K. Abbott).

'*I died*'. Innocence passed away.

'*Sin . . . beguiled me*'. Cf. 2 Cor 11³, with its reference to Eve. Through the commandment, he says, it '*slew me*'.

7¹²⁻¹³. The passage begins with a clause in an uncompleted sentence, probably intended to contrast the law and the commandment ('*holy, and righteous, and good*') with sin. But Paul breaks off to ask the question: '*Did then that which is good become death unto me?*' 'No, no' ('*God forbid*'), he says, it was '*sin working death to me through that which is good*'. Or '*by working*'.

'*that it might be shewn to be sin*' gives the reason for this perversion of the good, and it is further explained by the clause, '*that through the commandment sin might become exceeding sinful*'.

'*exceeding*', 'beyond measure'.

7¹⁴. From this point present tenses are used, in order vividly to depict the futility of the attempt to fulfil the demands of legal righteousness apart from the grace of God in Christ (cf. verse **25a**). This was Paul's experience in the past, and it is that of any man who attempts to do the same thing.

'*spiritual*', that is, in its nature and origin.

'*carnal*', that is possessing a nature in which sin is entrenched. Literally the word means 'fleshly'. But Paul is not speaking merely of his human nature in its frailty, nor, on the other hand, does he mean to suggest that it is evil in itself. His view is that in human nature self-regarding impulses and pride have their seat. They are in control. He is '*sold under sin*', that is, like a slave he is in bondage to it.

7¹⁵⁻¹⁶. '*For that which I do I know not*'. In other words: 'I am a mystery to myself.' Will and practice are at variance. Ovid's words, 'I see and approve the better; I follow the worse' (*Metamorphoses*, vii.19f), are often quoted in this connexion. With a backward glance to verse **12**, Paul adds, 'I (thereby) admit that the law is good'.

7¹⁷⁻¹⁸. He can only conclude that his will is enslaved: '*it is no more I . . . but sin which dwelleth in me*'. Nothing good, he affirms, dwells in his lower nature ('*in my flesh*'). Later, in verse **22**, he says that, in his higher self he delights in the law of God. His inner life is divided and therefore frustrated.

'*dwelleth*', or 'is at my command'.

7¹⁹⁻²⁰. '*For the good which I would I do not: but the evil which I would not, that I practise*'. Man's divided heart and spiritual impotence are powerfully described in these verses, and a second time reference is made to indwelling sin.

7²¹⁻³. '*I find then the law*'. Not the Mosaic Law, but an inner regulative principle. 'This is how things stand'.

'*after the inward man*', '*the inmost self*'='*my mind*' (verse **23**), the higher rational man.

'*a different law*', that is, principle.

'*in my members*'='*in my flesh*' (verse **18**).

This 'different principle' opposes and defeats his true self ('*the law of my mind*'), making it a captive to itself ('*the law of sin which is in my members*').

7²⁴. Out of this poignant situation arises the cry, '*O wretched man that I am!*', and the agonized question: '*who shall deliver me out of the body of this death?*'

'*the body of this death*'. Alternatively, 'this body of death', that is, 'this dead self'. Cf. **6⁶**, '*the body of sin*'.

It is improbable that in either passage Paul is thinking solely of the physical body. It is not from a mortal body that he asks to be delivered, but from a *self* menaced by spiritual death. See the Glossary and compare the use of the word '*bodies*' in **12¹**.

7²⁵ᵃ. God alone can deliver him '*through Jesus Christ our Lord*'.

'*I thank God*'. Among several variant readings the best attested seems to be 'Thanks be to God'. But Christ is the deliverer, not the medium of thanksgiving. Through Him God integrates and rescues the doomed self.

7²⁵ᵇ. Moffatt and some commentators think that originally this passage followed verse **23**, but there is no textual evidence in favour of this suggestion, and it does not seem necessary. The passage sums up the situation described in **7⁷⁻²⁴**.

'*I myself*' is very emphatic. Moffatt has 'left to myself' the *RSV* 'of myself'. C. L. Mitton suggests the paraphrase 'when I rely on my own resources, and cease to depend on God', pointing to the contrast in **8¹**, '*in Christ*'. See Dr Mitton's three articles, 'Romans 7 Reconsidered', *Exp. T.*, LXV.78-81, 99-103, 132-5.

'*with the mind*' (cf. **1²⁸, 7²³, 12²**), 'the inner self', the higher rational part of one's nature.

'*with the flesh*'. See the Glossary and the note on **7¹⁴**. The lower self dominated by sin is meant.

With the mind God's commands ('*the law of God*') are served; with the flesh the authority of sin ('*the law of sin*').

In the articles mentioned above Dr Mitton sums up his discussion as follows: 'We conclude, therefore, that Ro 7¹⁴⁻²⁵ is not meant to be either a description of Paul's pre-Christian experience, nor is it to be taken as a description of a "man in Christ". It is rather the description of a man who is trying to live the good life, but doing it in his own strength, relying on his own resources, whether the period in his life be before his conversion to Christ or after it, in a later period of "back-sliding", when through carelessness the absolutely essential "injection" of Divine power has been neglected', op. cit., p. 135.

Law and Grace is a theme which is relevant at all times, since the temptation to rely on oneself in seeking to fulfil moral codes of all kinds is always with us. The best way to expose this insidious peril is an expository treatment of 7¹⁴⁻²⁵ expressed in modern terms. Psychology has much to tell us about frustration and discord, the divided mind and inner conflict, and the sense of impotence which they bring. But in the nature of the case its helpfulness is limited, since sin is essentially a religious concept and deliverance through Christ is the distinctive Christian gospel. The warning that we are never safe from discord and the constant danger of lapsing into self-sufficiency, unconscious or half-conscious adherence to the legal principle in religion, even on the part of supposedly Christian people, preachers and hearers alike, the pride that lurks in the heart of the best of us, all these facts and considerations show the importance of Paul's teaching today and always. The passage 7²⁴⁻⁵, '*O wretched man that I am! who shall deliver me out of the body of this death? I thank God through Jesus Christ our Lord*', will always make its appeal to the preacher, as exposing man's deepest need and declaring the good news in Christ. It should, of course, be expounded in relation to its context from 7¹⁴ onwards, and briefly but clearly and connected with man's need today.

(10) 8¹⁻¹⁷: Life in the Spirit

This section is dominated by the thought of new life in the Holy Spirit, a life which manifests itself in freedom from the power of sin (8⁵⁻¹¹) and sonship with God (8¹²⁻¹⁷).

8¹⁻². The passage looks back to 7¹⁴⁻²⁵ and to the shout of joy in 7²⁵ in particular.

'*no condemnation*', in contrast with 5¹⁶, ¹⁸, and because '*sin in the flesh*' is condemned (verse 3).

'*Them that are in Christ Jesus*'. See the note on 6¹¹.

'*the law*'. This is one of the cases in which the word is used in the broader sense (cf. 7¹, ²¹, ²³). 'Authority' or 'rule' is meant. So also in the phrase '*the law of sin and of death*'.

'*the Spirit of life*' is the Spirit who gives life. The Spirit is mentioned about twenty times in this chapter.

'*in Christ Jesus*'. Cf. 6[11]. The phrase can be taken with '*the Spirit of life*' or with the verb '*made free*'.

8[3]. '*what the law could not do*'. The phrase is flung out like a caption, 'a thing impossible for the law' (C. F. D. Moule), to be followed by a dash. Alternatively, some commentators suggest that we should understand the verb 'did' (after 'God') and continue 'by sending . . . he condemned . . .'.

'*through the flesh*', that is, human nature possessed by evil impulses (cf. 7[23]).

'*his own son*'. Cf. 1[3-4], [9], 5[10], 8[29], [32]. '*Own*' is emphatic. Belief in the pre-existence of Christ is implied. Cf. Phil 2[6].

'*in the likeness of sinful flesh*'. Cf. Phil 2[7], '*in the likeness of men*'. No hesitation about the reality of Christ's humanity is implied. Paul is unable to say 'in the flesh', because for him 'flesh' is human nature in its frailty or as ruled by sin. See 7[14].

'*and as an offering for sin*. If the Greek is so read, the reference is to the 'sin-offering' (Lev 4[2-35]). But, although Paul interprets the death of Christ in sacrificial terms, he does not elsewhere mention the 'sin-offering' as the author of Hebrews does. It is better therefore to adopt the *RV*m rendering '*and for sin*' (cf. 3[25]). Cf. 1 Cor 15[3].

'*condemned sin in the flesh*, that is, passed sentence upon it.

It is important to notice that Paul's doctrine of the Atonement includes the Incarnation as well as the Crucifixion. So in Phil 2[6-8].

8[4]. '*the ordinance of the law*', that is, its commands. The statement that the requirement '*might be fulfilled*' is not strange in view of the words which follow, '*in us, who walk not after the flesh, but after the spirit*'. Paul has already spoken highly of the Mosaic Law *in itself* in 7[16], [22].

The antithesis of flesh and spirit is treated in verses **5-8**.

8[5-8]. The contrast is that between men when left to themselves and men who have received the power of the Spirit.

'*the mind of the flesh*', that is, the thoughts, feelings, and emotions of the 'natural' man. These embody an '*enmity*' against God which ends in death, since he does not, and cannot, obey His law.

'*the mind of the spirit*', the mind imparted by the Spirit. It issues, Paul says, in '*life*' and '*peace*'.

'*They that are in the flesh*', that is, the earth-bound, '*cannot please God*'. This statement prepares the way for verses **9-10.**

8⁹⁻¹⁰. What has just been said is now applied to the readers. They are '*not in the flesh*'; they are '*in the spirit*', since the Spirit dwells in them.

'*if so be*', or, more accurately, 'if, as is the case'. No doubt is expressed. No man, Paul affirms, belongs to Christ unless he has '*the Spirit of Christ*'.

'*the Spirit of God . . . the Spirit of Christ . . . . Christ*'. These different names are connected with one and the same experience. Paul does not identify Christ with the Spirit, not even in 2 Cor 3¹⁷, but the same functions are ascribed to both. The Spirit is also '*the Spirit of God*'. The work of the Spirit is fully personal.

'*And if Christ is in you*'. This condition dominates what follows.

'*the body is dead because of sin*'. '*the body*' is either the physical body doomed, in Paul's view, because of the sin of Adam (5¹²), or, more probably, the lower self virtually '*dead*' because sin has been condemned (8³). The '*mortal body*', intentionally so described, is treated in verse **11.**

'*The spirit is life because of righteousness*'. '*The spirit*' may be the new or higher self alive because of God's righteous activity in Christ, but is perhaps better interpreted as the Holy Spirit, who for the same reason imparts life.

The whole passage is obscure, as the history of exposition shows, but it is clearly intended as a description of a radical contrast between two very different levels of human experience, the 'natural' and the 'spiritual' life.

8¹¹. A further condition is laid down: the indwelling of the Spirit of God who raised Jesus from the dead.

'*your mortal bodies* . Clearly, the physical body is meant. The presence of the adjective '*mortal*' is felt to be necessary because '*soma*' ('body') does not always bear this meaning. See the Glossary. (Significantly enough '*soma*' is never used by Paul with the meaning 'corpse'.)

'*shall quicken*', that is, 'make alive', 'cause to live', 'give life to' (*RSV*). Cf. what is said in 1 Cor 15⁴⁴⁻⁹ and 2 Cor 5¹⁻⁴ of the '*spiritual body*', the fitting organ of the new life.

8¹²⁻¹³. We are under an obligation, therefore, not to live '*after the flesh*', for then we must die, but, it is implied, '*after the Spirit*'.

'*the deeds of the body*', those of the fleshly self (cf. **6⁵, ¹⁹** and **7²⁴**). The ambiguity is due to the lack of an adequate psychological terminology.

'*mortify*', that is, 'make to die' (*RV*m), not of ourselves, but '*by the spirit*', that is, the Holy Spirit.

8¹⁴⁻¹⁵. A new theme, Sonship, is now introduced. Those who are guided by the Spirit are '*the sons of God*'. A new status is given to them. Cf. Luke 6³⁵.

'*the spirit of bondage*', the temper and outlook of a slave.

'*the spirit of adoption*', the mind of a son.

The former expresses itself in '*fear*', the latter in the liturgical cry: '*Abba, Father*.'

'*Abba, Father*'. '*Abba*' is the Aramaic word for '*Father*', here supplied in the Greek text. Derived from the prayer of Jesus in Gethsemane (Mark 14³⁶), the ejaculation must have been common in the public worship of the bilingual communities of primitive Christianity. Cf. the use of the Aramaic expression, '*Marana tha*', Our Lord, come' (1 Cor 16²²). See the note on **1⁴**.

'*adoption*'. Deissmann, *Bible Studies*, p. 239, has shown how common the practice of adoption was in the world of Paul's day. Paul applies the name '*son*' only to believers, but this usage does not exclude the conviction (not attested by Paul or John) that potentially all men are God's sons. Such was the belief of Jesus (cf. Luke 15²⁴). There is a great difference, however, between potential and real sonship, and it is to this that Paul refers when he says '*Ye received the spirit of adoption*'. The word has a legal sound, but Paul's meaning is anything but legal. The ejaculation '*Abba*' shows that he is thinking of a tender, personal relationship realized in the joy of adoring worship.

8¹⁶⁻¹⁷. As John Wesley taught, Paul insists that there is a witness of '*the Spirit himself*' with our spirit that '*we are children of God*'. Here the more tender word, *teknon*, is used.

'*if children*', Paul exults, '*then heirs*; *heirs of God*, *and joint-heirs with Christ*', if, as is the case (cf. verse **9**), '*we suffer with*

him, that we may be also glorified with him'. Cf. 2 Cor 1[7],
Phil 3[10], *'the fellowship of his sufferings'*. This suffering involves
a sharing in His redemptive sufferings. Cf. Col 1[24].

The principal themes of the section are New Life in the Spirit and
Sonship with God. Both are timely today in view of man's sense of
frustration and defeat, and the danger of losing the individual in
the crowd. That men can be lifted out of themselves into new life
by the power of the Spirit and can become sons of God in truth are
the enheartening notes of a living gospel. In presenting these
themes the doctrine of the Spirit demands study and calls for an
exposition of biblical teaching concerning the Spirit, as the personal
life-giving power of God, raising men above themselves and their
circumstances, banishing the sense of futility, and witnessing to the
reality of divine sonship. Where else, save in the New Testament,
are these vital beliefs to be found? Among passages in the section
some of the most important texts are 8[1], *'There is therefore now no
condemnation to them that are in Christ'*, 8[14], *'For as many as are
led by the Spirit of God, these are sons of God'*, 8[16], *'The Spirit himself beareth witness with our spirit, that we are children of God'*.
In 8[15], *'Ye received the spirit of adoption, whereby we cry, Abba,
Father'*, one of the most interesting suggestions in recent years is
that of J. Jeremias, who shows that, while *Abba* was used by the
Jews in addressing a human father (but not of God), Jesus boldly
appropriated the word for use as a Divine name. Cf. *The Parables
of Jesus*, p. 134, and the account I have given of his arguments in
The Person of Christ in New Testament Teaching, pp. 177f.

(11) 8[18-30]: The Glory that is to be

Although again and again Paul emphasizes the present aspects of
salvation, his thought is incurably eschatological. It inevitably
turns, that is to say, to the culmination and end of all things.

In the present section the key-note is struck in the words, *'the
glory which shall be revealed to us-ward'*, and it is re-echoed in the
closing words in 8[30], *'them he also glorified'*. Words and phrases
like *'earnest expectation'*, *'hope'*, *'the firstfruits of the Spirit'*, *'waiting'*, *'patience'* (endurance), and *'firstborn'* illustrate this interest,
which takes the widest sweep, embracing nature itself as well as
man.

8[18]. In contemporary Jewish thought *'this present time'* or
'age' was sharply distinguished from *'the age to come'*; *'sufferings'* belong to the one, *'glory'*, the splendour of God's presence,

to the other; and between them there is no comparison. Such is Paul's assurance.

8¹⁹. '*earnest expectation*', a single word in the Greek to describe the attitude of stretching forward with the head thrust out. Here it is used of the created world.

'*the creation*'. The word, which otherwise means the act of creating, is here used of nature as a whole. Paul is conscious of a certain tension in nature corresponding to the tension in man. He interprets it as a waiting for '*the revealing of the sons of God*', their corporate manifestation as such at the Parousia, or coming, of Christ.

'*waiteth for*' translates an expressive verb which pictures a tense attitude of looking forward.

8²⁰⁻¹. The belief that nature was subjected to '*vanity*' (or futility) '*not of its own will*' is derived from Gen 3¹⁷⁻¹⁹. It corresponds to an acute sense of imperfection which many feel today. Paul has his own explanation. The futility, he holds, was imposed upon nature by God ('*by reason of him who subjected it*'), and '*in hope*' that, delivered from the slavery of corruption, it might share in '*the liberty of the glory of the children of God*'.

Some theologians have held the view that there must have been a pre-historic fall which has affected nature and made it brutal or irrational. This idea is speculative, and only moves the problem a stage further back. Paul appears to have felt the pathos of nature's 'thraldom to decay' (to use Moffatt's translation) and to have believed that the universe is to share in man's redemption.

For Jewish beliefs see 2 Esdras 7⁷⁵, 13²⁶. See also Isa 55²⁻¹³, 65¹⁷, Rev 21¹.

8²². This belief, or intuition, rests on a factual basis, the pain and suffering so manifest now in nature. The figure behind the references to groaning and travailing in pain is that of childbirth. Moffatt's translation is 'the entire creation sighs and throbs with pain'.

8²³. To this groaning there is a parallel in the Christian experience. Although the believer has received the gift of the Spirit, it is only '*the firstfruits*' that he enjoys, or, as Paul says elsewhere, '*the earnest*' (or first instalment) of the Spirit (2 Cor 1²², 5⁵; cf. Eph 1¹⁴). He awaits a completed '*adoption*' in the deliverance of his body.

'*the redemption of our body*'. Here, as in 8¹¹, Paul is thinking of a renewed '*spiritual body*' (cf. 1 Cor 15⁴⁴), the organ of a perfected sonship. So far is he from thinking of resurrection as mere resuscitation! Cf. 2 Cor 5¹, 'We know that if the earthly house of our tabernacle be dissolved, we have a building from God, a house not made with hands, eternal, in the heavens'. The whole passage, 2 Cor 5¹⁻⁴, is of the greatest interest.

8²⁴⁻⁵. Salvation, he explains, was '*in hope*', a better translation than '*by hope*'.

'*Patience*', or better, 'endurance', is the manner and spirit in which we hope for what as yet is not seen. The word Paul uses describes an active patience, the endurance of which Jesus spoke as that by which we win our souls (Luke 21¹⁹).

8²⁶⁻⁷. '*in like manner*'. To the groaning of nature and of man Paul sees a parallel in the groaning of the Spirit.

'*helpeth our infirmity*', 'holds us in support'.

In praying we know not what to pray, that is, how to word our prayers, but the Spirit intercedes for us in unutterable words known only to God.

'*maketh intercession for us*'. Much is lost in modern Christianity by the neglect of this truth. See also 8³⁴. Intercession is not wheedling or persuading God to be gracious, but a ministry on high for us in our inarticulateness. The astonishing and comforting truth in Paul's statement is that, in His divine compassion, the Spirit Himself shares in our wordless prayers '*with groanings which cannot be uttered*'. But the Searcher of hearts knows the Spirit's intention ('*mind*').

'*because*'. But the word can also be rendered 'that'. God knows that the Spirit's intercession is for '*the saints*' (cf. 1⁷), and that He intercedes in accordance with His will.

8²⁸. A further ground for confidence is the fact that God causes all things to work together for good for those who love Him.

'*all things work together for good*'. But important textual authorities insert, as the subject, 'God': 'God works all things

together', or, alternatively, 'co-operates in all things for good'
(C. H. Dodd). A divine activity, not an automatic process, is
described. This agrees with what follows.

'*to them that are called according to his purpose*'. For Paul's
emphasis on election, or calling, see the note on 1¹. The
phrase further characterizes those for whom God makes all
things work together, those, namely, that love God.

'*to them that love God*'. This is one of Paul's rare allusions
to *our* love for God (or Christ). Cf. 1 Cor 2⁹, 8³, 16²², Eph 6²⁴.
See J. Moffatt, *Love in the New Testament*, pp. 154-63. And
even here the further definition noted above is important.
Those who love God are not arbitrarily selected, but they are
'*called*' by Him. See further verse **30**.

8²⁹. '*For whom he foreknew, he also foreordained*'.

'*foreordained*', or 'predestined', 'predetermined'.

Later doctrines of predestination, including reprobation,
must not prevent us from recognizing Paul's insistence upon
the fact that believers are known, destined, and called by
God eternally. This idea corresponds in part with our experience; for, looking back, we see that, apart from our response
in faith, we had nothing to do with our salvation. And even
faith is '*the gift of God*' (Eph 2⁸). All is of God. It is of vital
importance to observe to *what* we are predestinated. Paul
never speaks of predestination to damnation.

'*to be conformed to the image of his Son*'. This, and nothing
less is the end in view.

'*conformed*', that is, 'made like in form'. Cf. Phil 3²¹,
2 Cor 3¹⁸.

'*image*' is more than 'likeness'; it denotes the facsimile or
basic pattern.

'*of his Son*', who is himself '*the image of God*' (2 Cor 4⁴,
Col 1¹⁵; cf. Heb 1³). For '*his Son*' see the note on 1³.

'*that he might be the firstborn among many brethren*'. Cf.
Col 1¹⁸. The word '*firstborn*' is here used, not as in Col 1¹⁵ to
describe the absolute supremacy of Christ, but His place as
the head of a great brotherhood. The Christian is predestined
to likeness to Christ and fellowship within His community.

8³⁰. In this climax to the section the believer's destiny is
further unfolded. '*Foreordained*', we were '*called*' (cf. verse **28**);

E

'*called*', we were '*justified*' (cf. 3²⁴); '*justified*', we were '*glorified*'. The astonishing thing in this mounting catalogue is the past tense of '*he also glorified*', when the theme of the whole is the glory that is to be. G. G. Findlay described it as 'the most daring anticipation of faith even the N.T. contains'. Even now that which shall be is present in part.

The hope which glows all through this section of the Epistle is especially timely today, when man is less confident of his ability to bring in the New Age, and is tempted to relapse into pessimism. It is the preacher's privilege to unfold this hope, which is grounded from first to last in God, and not in man; to point out the realism which looks steadily at the signs of frustration in nature as well as in man, and yet does not yield to despair; and to make clear the spiritual foundations on which this confidence can rest, in (1) the ceaseless ministry of the Holy Spirit, and (2) the eternal purpose of God for man. We are mistaken if we think that Predestination, Election, Justification, and Glorification are topics which belong only to the past. All have a present and a future significance, since it is for lovers of God, in whom He fulfils His sovereign purposes, that He makes all things work together for good. Hope in things not seen, and the endurance which goes with hope centred in the Living God, is the message needed for '*men fainting for fear, and for expectation of the things which are coming on the world*' (Luke 21²⁶). If 8²⁸ is chosen as a text, it should be presented in the form, 'With those who love God, God co-operates in all things for good', as explained in the note above. See *NEB*.

(12) 8³¹⁻⁹: The Certainty of God's Purposes

All through the Epistle Paul has objections and difficulties in mind. Here, in this section, he combats the doubts which assail the Christian Hope, ending with an impassioned testimony to the all-sufficiency of the Love of Christ for us, a testimony which is without parallel in the world's literature.

8³¹⁻². '*What then shall we say to these things?*' The odds may indeed seem against us. Paul disdains the odds. True to himself, he stakes all upon God. '*If God is for us, who is against us?*'

Not content with a challenge, he points to what God has done in the gift of His own Son, recalling in his language Abraham's readiness to sacrifice Isaac (Gen 22¹⁶).

'*He that*', or, more literally, 'The same One who'.

'*delivered him up for us all*'. Paul took over this teaching, which reflects Isa 53, from the earliest preaching. Cf. Acts 2²³.

'*how shall he not also with him freely give us all things?*' Granting the saving act of God, which no Christian can doubt, the logic is irrefutable.

'*all things*'. Those mentioned in 8¹⁸⁻³⁰, especially '*the glory that shall be revealed to us-ward*'.

8³³⁻⁴. But are we really secure? As Paul puts it: '*Who shall lay anything to the charge of God's elect?*'

The reply 'No one' is implied in the words, '*It is God that justifieth*', which mean that He, as Judge, has already treated us as righteous. There is no other tribunal, save His, to fear!

But are we not after all exposed to condemnation? 'No' is again implied in the fact that Christ died, rose again, is exalted on high, and makes intercession for us.

'*maketh intercession for us*'. The same ministry of intercession is ascribed to Christ as that of the Spirit (8²⁷). As in the case of the session '*at the right hand of God*' the language is necessarily pictorial, but the truth is infinitely precious.

> *Christ is our Advocate on high;*
> *Thou art our Advocate within.*

The same idea appears in the Epistle to the Hebrews in 7²⁵, 'seeing he ever liveth to make intercession', and in 9²⁻⁴, 'now to appear before the face of God for us', and again in 1 Jn 2¹, 'We have an Advocate with the Father'.

Otherwise than in the above exposition, the punctuation of the *RV* suggests that the answer to the question about the elect is '*It is God that justifieth; who is he that shall condemn?*' That is, a statement is followed by a challenging question. Similarly, the statement about Christ in verse **34** is followed by the question in **35**. It seems better, however, to interpret '*who is he that shall condemn?*' as a separate and parallel question, to which **34** supplies the answer. A still further question in **35f.** is answered in **37**.

If 8³³⁻⁴ is read in this way, the translation will run, 'Who shall lay anything to the charge of God's elect? (No one.) God is the one who justifies. Who is he that shall condemn? (For) it is Christ Jesus who died . . . who also makes intercession for us. Who shall separate us from the love of Christ?

Shall tribulation . . . ? Nay, in all these things we are more than conquerors . . .'.

The *RV*m, '*Shall Christ Jesus that died, . . . us?*' (so *RSV*), does not seem necessary.

8[35-7]. '*Who*', Paul asks, '*shall separate us from the love of Christ?*' Tribulation, anguish, persecution, famine, nakedness, peril, and sword are all mentioned as possibilities, and a parallel is seen in the words of Ps 44[22].

'*the love of Christ*'. Undoubtedly, His love for us. Some MSS, probably influenced by verse **39**, read 'God'.

The dangers are recognized, but the possibility of being overcome is scouted. '*In all these things we are more than conquerors*', but '*through him that loved us*'.

8[38-9]. This glowing climax mentions every adversary Paul can think of and denies that any of them can separate us from '*the love of God, which is in Christ Jesus our Lord*'.

'*I am persuaded*'. The Greek tense implies a conviction reached and still maintained.

'*nor angels, nor principalities, . . . nor powers*'. These three names describe hostile supernatural beings feared in Paul's day and recognized, although not feared, by the Apostle himself. Cf. 1 Cor 15[24], Col 2[10], Eph 1[21]. In the rush of Paul's eloquence '*powers*' are mentioned separately.

'*nor things present, nor things to come*'. Paul may be thinking of experiences like those mentioned in 1 Cor 4[9-13] and 2 Cor 11[23-9].

'*nor height, nor depth*'. These terms are probably not merely spatial, but allusions to the home of elementary spirits (cf. Gal 4[3, 9], Col 2[8, 20]) supposed to inhabit the stars, and to demons of the abyss (cf. Luke 8[31], Rev 9[1], etc.).

'*nor any other creature*', that can be conceived or imagined. None of these, Paul is convinced, can drive a wedge between ourselves and God's love. When he says that this love is '*in Christ Jesus our Lord*', he means that it is manifested in Him and in all that He does for us. Chapters **5, 6,** and **8** all end in a reference to '*our Lord*'. This phrase was not only luminous to the readers in their personal experience, but was also brought powerfully to their minds in the worship of the community and especially in the Christian Eucharist (cf. 1 Cor 11[23-6]).

Christian Certainty is the main theme of the section. It has gained in its urgency after the shattering experiences of two world wars and amid the fears and frustrations of the post-war period. Paul tells us that we have no security at all save in the Love of God. This is the corner-stone of his theology. This belief does not mean that we may neglect political activity or stand aside from attempts to secure international goodwill; but his teaching does expose the futility of all human efforts and undertakings based on anything less than a universal sharing in the Love of God in Christ.

The threefold foundation of authority in Christian belief is the Word of God, the historic witness of the Church, and the realities of the Christian experience. All these testify to the Love of God, and each calls for that God-inspired response of the human spirit which is faith or dependence upon God. Well-meaning attempts to short-circuit this conception of Christian assurance by insisting upon the infallibility of the Bible or of the Church are futile. Both are of supreme importance, but as media through which the spirit speaks. In the end our only security is in God and in what He has done and still is. But this is security enough.

The Bible tells us about God and what He has done for us in history and especially in Christ, our Lord. And the Church has summarized what Christians believe in the Creeds. In this respect they are buttresses of faith, although not the foundation stone itself. The foundation stone is Christ, as Paul declares in Eph 2[20], 'Christ Jesus himself being the chief corner stone'. Cf. 1 Pet 2[5-6].

Perhaps the best way of treating the question of Religious Certainty is a sermon followed by a discussion class, for many questions arise in the minds of hearers which cannot be fully treated by a preacher in the time at his disposal.

THREE

God's Purposes for Jew and Gentile

9^1-11^{36}. The heading 'The Rejection of the Jews' under which these chapters are often considered is not satisfactory since other important themes are introduced including the teaching concerning works and faith, the mercy shown to the Gentiles, and the final restoration of the Jews. Moreover, while 'the casting away' of the Jews is mentioned in 11^{15} in contrast with their 'receiving', it is expressly denied in 11^1 that God has repudiated His people. Paul affirms that 'a hardening in part hath befallen Israel, until the fullness of the Gentiles be come in' (11^{25}), and it is with anguish of heart that he discusses this, the causes which have brought it about, and the problems it raises regarding the fulfilment of God's purposes for the world.

It has been suggested that these three chapters were written apart from the rest of the Epistle, perhaps as a sermon. This conjecture may be sound, but in any case the section stands in organic connexion with the rest of the Epistle. It discusses the same themes; promise and election, legal righteousness and that which is of faith, grace and mercy, but particularly in their historical aspects as seen in the history of Israel, past, present, and future. The deep feeling which pervades the section, especially in 9^{1-5}, is manifest to every reader. Paul's heart is torn as he thinks of the failure of Israel to attain righteousness sought with such zeal, but in the wrong way, yet he is unwavering in his insistence on the divine sovereignty and exults in wonder at God's grace which, in spite of disobedience, brings His purposes for men to pass.

After the introduction (9^{1-5}) the chapters fall into three main sections: (1) 9^{6-29}, which discusses God's process of selection in the fulfilment of His purposes, His justice, and His mercy towards the elect; (2) 9^{30}-10^{21}, which grapples with the question, 'Why did Israel fail?; and (3) 11^{1-32}, which traces the consequences of the hardening of Israel in the salvation which came to the Gentiles, and looks forward to the restoration of the Jews by God who 'never goes back upon his gifts and His call' (Moffatt).

9^{1-5}: Paul's Anguish as He thinks of the Privileges of Israel

9^{1-3}. Paul's strong insistence that he is speaking *'the truth in*

Christ', not lying, and that his conscience bears witness with him '*in the Holy Ghost*', implies that he is well aware of charges of disloyalty to his own kinsmen, the Jews. These charges may have been current even within the Roman community.

He protests that he has '*great sorrow*' and '*unceasing pain*' in his heart, and could even pray to be '*anathema from Christ*' his '*brethren's sake*'.

'*I could wish*'. The Greek word means 'pray'. Paul has in mind the prayer of Moses: 'Yet now, if thou wilt forgive their sin—; and if not, blot me, I pray thee, out of thy book which thou hast written' (Ex 32³²).

'*anathema*'. Cf. Acts 23¹⁴, 1 Cor 12³, 16²², Gal 1⁸·⁹. The word denotes something or someone placed under a ban for destruction, 'accursed'. The pronoun 'I' is made emphatic, literally 'I of myself'; cf. 7²⁵ᵇ.

'*my brethren's sake*'. The word '*brethren*' used of fellow Christians is applied to the Jews.

'*according to the flesh*', that is, on the physical side. Cf. 1³ 9⁵.

9⁴⁻⁵. The immense privileges of the Jews are now described.

'*Israelites*'. The name of privilege. Cf. Eph 2¹².

'*the adoption*'. The status of legal sonship. Cf. Ex 4²²ᶠ, Jer 31⁹.

'*the glory*'. Called later the Shekinah, the visible presence of God; cf. Ex 16¹⁰.

'*the covenants*'. Cf. Gen 15¹⁸, 17²· ⁷· ⁹, Ex 2²⁴.

'*the giving of the law*'. The Mosaic Law.

'*the service of God*', that is, the Temple worship.

'*the promises*'. The divine promises, especially those discussed in 4¹³⁻²⁰.

'*the fathers*'. Abraham, Isaac, Jacob, etc.

'*Christ*'. Probably in this catalogue of privileges we should read 'the Messiah'. For '*according to the flesh*' (*RSV*) see 1³, 9³.

'*who is over all, God blessed for ever*'. So rendered the phrase denotes the deity of Christ. So many commentators. But nowhere else does Paul call Christ 'God'. In Phil 2⁶ he speaks of Him as 'being in the form of God' and as renouncing or refusing to grasp, 'equality with God'. Probably, with many other commentators, we should place a full stop after

'Christ', and read what follows as a doxology, 'God who is over all be blessed for ever'; or alternatively, put a stop after 'over all', reading 'God be blessed for ever'. A doxology after the list of privileges is appropriate.

(1)   9⁶⁻²⁹: The Divine Sovereignty in Judgement

Paul denies that the word of God has come to nought, since the promises were not made to the people as a whole. A process of selection is manifest in the history of Israel, in the choice of Isaac and Jacob. In this God is not unjust, since His will is sovereign. The case of Pharaoh is a case in point. God has mercy on whom He wills and whom He wills He hardens. Man must not presume to question His will. That which is formed cannot say to the one who formed it: 'Why did you make me so?' The potter has the right to make what he will with his clay. A different point is made in 9²²⁻⁹, namely, that God endured with much longsuffering people deserving of destruction, in order to show mercy to the elect among Jews and Gentiles. This action is in accordance with the prophecy of Hosea, 'I will call that my people which was not my people', and with Isaiah's words about the saving of a remnant.

Much in this section raises almost insuperable difficulties in the mind of the modern reader. Man is not passive clay in the hands of a potter. The utter sovereignty of God is emphasized to such a degree that no room seems left for human freedom. It will not do with Nygren (*Commentary on Romans*, p. 369) to say that 'a theodicy assumes that *man* is central'. God is not a Celestial Sultan. What the reader must do is to understand the section, and Paul's dilemma. He does not write as a philosopher, but as one whose heart is torn as he contemplates the apparent frustration of the purposes of God. And we must not miss his emphasis upon the longsuffering of God and the existence of a remnant.

9⁶⁻⁷. *'For they are not all Israel, which are of Israel'*. It is on this fact that Paul fixes in maintaining that the word of God has not failed. The promise made to Abraham was *'in Isaac shall thy seed be called'* (Gen 21¹²).

9⁸⁻⁹. From this passage it is deduced that physical descent alone is not a sufficient ground for inheriting the promise. The *'children of God'* (that is, although this is not stated in so many words, those who are chosen by Him) belong to the true succession. These are '*reckoned for a seed*', that is, as Abraham's descendants. The point of the quotation which follows (cf. Gen 18$^{10, 14}$) is that the birth of Isaac was supernatural; it was the result of a divine promise.

9$^{9-13}$. '*And not only so*', Paul continues. Not all Isaac's descendants inherited the promise. Jacob was chosen instead of Esau.

The sentence beginning '*but Rebecca also*' is broken off and resumed in another manner in verse **12,** the intervening verse (**11**) forming a parenthesis. The awkwardness of the construction is caused by Paul's desire to show that the choice of Jacob was due solely to God's purpose '*according to election*'. It was made before the children were born, as the passage quoted (Gen 25^{23}) shows, not because of their conduct.

The second quotation, '*Jacob I loved, but Esau I hated*', is from Mal 1$^{2-3}$. Commentators often soften the difficulty of the quotation by saying that it refers to the nations, the Jews and the Edomites, but it may be doubted if this is Paul's thought. Probably he interpreted the passage literally in accordance with his desire to insist on the complete freedom of God's choice.

'*that the purpose of God according to election might stand, not of works, but of him that calleth*'. This is the key passage in Paul's argument. God's action, he means, is His own, and is in no way determined by human merit ('*not of works*'). He is not thinking of predestination to salvation or damnation, as Calvin taught, but of God's choice of the line of succession in which the promise made to Abraham might be fulfilled. Manifestly, his intention is to show that His action in calling the Gentiles is in line with the principle of divine selection illustrated in the history of Israel.

9^{14}. Paul realizes that his historical survey raises the question, 'Is God just?'

'*unrighteousness*' is here used in its ethical sense, namely, of wrongdoing. That God is unjust he strongly denies.

9$^{15-16}$. These verses contain Paul's answer; they are not a further development of the objection. Ex 33^{19} is quoted, '*I will have mercy on whom I have mercy . . .*'. The argument is that God is entirely free to show mercy and compassion on whomsoever He wills to do so. In no way is He dependent upon man's will or action.

'*it*' is the exercise of mercy.

'*not of him that willeth, nor of him that runneth*'. These phrases refer to man's activity. Paul frequently uses the figure of running, derived from the public games, in this sense; cf. 1 Cor 9²⁴, ²⁶, Phil 2¹⁶, Gal 2², 5⁷. The positive statement follows, '*but of God that hath mercy*'.

9¹⁷⁻¹⁸. '*For the scripture saith unto Pharaoh*', The scripture is mentioned with intention, as an authority which no Jewish objector would question. The reference is to Ex 9¹⁶.

It may seem strange that, after stating God's prerogative in the exercise of mercy, Paul should cite an example of judgement and hardening. In this, however, he is logical, since in his view God's sovereignty extends in both directions, in mercy and in judgement. Cf. 1²⁴, ²⁶, ²⁸.

'*For this very purpose did I raise thee up*'. The reference is not, as in the Hebrew and Greek Bibles, to Pharaoh's restoration from sickness, but to God's act in bringing him on the stage of history in order to show His power and to make Himself known in all the earth. As the next verse **(18)** shows, Paul has in mind the statement repeated in Exodus (4²¹, 9¹², 11¹⁰, 14⁴) that the Lord '*hardened Pharaoh's heart*'.

'*So then he hath mercy on whom he will, and whom he will he hardeneth*'. In these words Paul sums up his immediate argument.

The modern reader will not, in most cases, be able to sympathize with this austere emphasis upon the sovereignty of God, so far at least as 'hardening' is concerned. But he ought not to try to soften it or explain it away. It represents a point of view common to Paul and the Jewish teachers of his day due to the tendency to find the primary cause of all things in God to the neglect of what we today recognize as secondary causes. See the note on 1²⁴. The attempt to take Paul's teaching as it stands is responsible both for the higher and the lower elements in Calvinism, the true sovereignty of God and the doctrine of reprobation. For a modern attempt to defend Paul's teaching, see Nygren, *Commentary on Romans*, pp. 364-74.

Paul himself is conscious of the objections which might be brought against his teaching, as may be seen in verses **19-21** and in his endeavour to show that the ultimate purpose of God is mercy in verses **22-4**.

9¹⁹. Paul states the objection which the reader may raise: *'Why doth he still find fault? For who withstandeth his will?'* It cannot be said that he answers this objection. It really amounts to the question, how can God condemn one whom He has hardened?

9²⁰⁻¹. His reply is a protest against human presumption. The questions ought not to be asked! We are but clay in the hands of the potter and have no right to ask: *'Why didst thou make me thus?'* C. H. Dodd, *The Epistle of Paul to the Romans*, p. 139, justly says: 'It is the weakest point in the whole epistle.' Man is not as clay in the hands of a potter; he has freedom. If challenged, Paul would probably have recognized this, for the co-existence of predestination and human freedom were frankly recognized by contemporary Jewish teachers, but were not reconciled, as modern theologians cannot reconcile them, apart from an appeal to God's over-ruling activity. For Jewish teaching Josephus, *Antiquities*, xiii. 5, 9, is often quoted. For the analogy of the potter see Isa 64⁸, Jer 18⁶.

9²²⁻³. The obscurity of this passage is probably a sign that Paul is tentatively reaching out to a better answer.

'What if God . . .' . This conditional clause is not completed and perhaps intentionally so. There is a parallel in Luke 13⁹, but it is obscured in the English version by the addition of the word 'well' which is not represented in the Greek. The vine-dresser says of the fruitless vine, *'If it shall bear fruit thence-forth'*! or more freely rendered, 'Perchance it may yet bear fruit'! So Paul is saying: 'It may be that God . . . endured . . . *and that he might make known the riches of his glory upon vessels of mercy . . .'*! That is, His ultimate purpose is mercy. This interpretation is confirmed by what he says later concerning the restoration of Israel.

'willing'. The Greek participle can be rendered either 'because willing' or 'although willing'. The latter, with many commentators, is to be preferred.

'to shew his wrath, and to make his power known'. The phrase describes God's action in judgement.

'*endured with much longsuffering*' describes what God actually did in His dealings with the Jews.

'*vessels of wrath fitted unto destruction*'. The phrase is meant to describe the Jews, and is chosen in view of the language used in verse **21**, '*one part a vessel unto honour, and another unto dishonour*'. Similarly, '*vessels of mercy*' describes the elect.

'*and that*'. '*and*' is omitted by *Codex Vaticanus* and other authorities. The *RSV* omits it. Many commentators think it should be read because its omission makes the construction easier. It may, however, have been inserted to make '*endured*' **(22)** and '*make known*' **(23)** parallel. With its omission (on the whole to be preferred) '*that*' (literally 'in order that') introduces the main purpose of the enduring and the long-suffering. This is to make known '*the riches of his glory upon vessels of mercy*'.

'*vessels of mercy*' describes people (identified in the next verse) who are the *objects* of God's mercy, just as '*vessels of wrath*' speaks of those who are the *objects* of His wrath.

'*which he afore prepared unto glory*'. Here a divine activity is mentioned, in contrast with the previous phrase '*fitted unto destruction*', which describes the character of the vessels in question ('suited for', 'ripe for'). To use a similar phrase of the '*vessels of mercy*' would suggest that they are deserving of God's glory. It is in the interests of his conviction that 'all is of grace' that Paul says that God prepared them before-hand for this destiny. He does not mean to assert that attain-ment is fixed by an immutable decree so that it is inevitable, just as he avoids the suggestion of reprobation by the use of '*fitted for destruction*'. We cannot but feel that Paul is still embarrassed by his use of the analogy of the potter.

'*And that he might make known the riches of his glory*'. Behind the obscurity of the language there is an invaluable truth implicit in this phrase, namely that attainment, the splendour of the vision of God, is meant and prepared for. We enter into a heritage of grace. Cf. Eph 2[10].

9[24]. Paul explicitly identifies the '*vessels of mercy*'. '*Us*,' he says, '*whom he also called*' (cf. 8[30]), and he states what has been already implicit from 9[6] onwards, '*not from the Jews only, but also from the Gentiles*'. These are '*the children of the promise*' who '*are reckoned for a seed*' (9[8]).

9[25-6]. From this point onward Paul supports his argument by scripture quotations in the manner adopted by the Jewish Rabbis.

First he quotes Hos 2[23], reversing the clauses and reading the verb 'to love' instead of 'to have mercy'. To a daughter Hosea gave the significant name Lo-Ruhamah ('Un-loved') and to a son Lo-Ammi ('Not-my-people') as descriptive of the ten tribes, and in the passage quoted by Paul speaks of their restoration. Paul applies the prophecy to the Gentiles, as some Rabbis did.

The second quotation (verse **26**) is also from Hosea (1[10]).

'*in the place where it was said*' in the prophecy means Jerusalem, but for Paul it is the reversal of status which is important. It is for this reason that he quotes the prophet's words, '*And it shall be, that in the place where it was said unto them, Ye are not my people, there shall they be called sons of the living God*'.

9[27-9]. The next two quotations are from Isa 10[22.3] and Isa 1[9].

The first speaks of '*the remnant*', thus showing that the promise to Israel does not extend to all the people, and the second has the same meaning.

'*finishing it and cutting it short*'. Translators differ considerably in rendering the Greek phrase: 'fully and swiftly' (Boylan); 'with rigor and dispatch' (*RSV*, cf. Moffatt); 'a sentence conclusive and concise' (Sanday and Headlam).

A preacher who chooses a text from Chapter **9** is a bold man. But the times call for courage, and those who make a close study of the chapter (a cursory reading is useless) are amply rewarded. The passionate readiness of Paul to be '*anathema from Christ*' and the perils of privilege, are moving topics at all times (9[3-5]), but the section 9[6-29], although less attractive, is full of suggestiveness. 'Has the word of God failed?' is a burning question still, and Valid Succession is still politically and ecclesiastically relevant. The Purpose of God according to Election is no exploded myth, but a principle always operative which cries out for interpretation. No less true is the importance of God's Sovereign Will to have Mercy, provided more than a sentimental treatment of the theme is given. The longsuffering of God (for nations, Churches, and individuals) is a moving thought, which chastens and stings men if rightly expounded, and is relevant both for the preacher and his congregation. Have we given enough attention to that Preparation for Glory which precedes the response of faith? Or, in evangelistic activity, have we said more about giving ourselves to God than of His gifts to us, stressing our doing more than our heritage? Lastly, the doctrine of the Remnant, from which all pride is excluded, taught by Jesus as well as by Isaiah and Paul, rises before the mind with all its comfort and power as a theme which it is a preacher's privilege and responsibility to expound.

(2) 9³⁰-10²¹: Why Israel failed

If, in reading 9⁶⁻²⁹, we inclined to think that the sovereignty of God is pressed too far, to the neglect of human freedom, we find the balance redressed in the present section. We see also the justification for refusing to read more into what Paul says about '*the purpose of God according to election*' than his words convey and the need to supply qualifications which he does not stay to introduce and consider.

In 9³⁰-10²¹ Paul shows that Israel failed, not in fulfilment of a divine decree, but because righteousness was sought by works and not by faith, that she heard, but did not pay attention to the prophetic word, '*Whosoever shall call upon the name of the Lord shall be saved*', but was found to be 'a disobedient and gainsaying people'. Zeal for God was not matched by knowledge. The Jews did not subject themselves '*to the righteousness of God*'.

9³⁰⁻¹. In answer to his question, '*What shall we say then?*' Paul sums up the tragic situation of Jew and Gentile. Gentiles, without aiming at being right with God, attained it by faith; Jews, pursuing it by a rule of life, failed.

'*the righteousness which is of faith*'. See the note on 1¹⁷.

Alternatively, but with less probability, a second question is asked: 'Shall we say that . . . ?' On the whole it seems probable that Paul is giving his answer to the question, '*What shall we say then?*'

'*a law*' seems used here in the sense of a rule or code.

9³²⁻³. The answer to the question, '*Wherefore?*' (or 'Why?'). Literally rendered, it runs, 'Because, not by faith, but by works, they stumbled . . .', but probably we should understand, 'they pursued it' with 'not by faith, but by works', and take 'they stumbled . . .' as a further answer.

'*They stumbled at the stone of stumbling*'. This obscure statement becomes clear if we remember that the first Christians, even before Paul, thought of Christ as 'the Stone',

meaning the stone referred to in Isa 8[14] and Isa 28[16], which
as here quoted are fused together. The same passages are
quoted in 1 Pet 2[6, 8], and in 1 Pet 2[7] a similar 'stone-passage'
is quoted from Ps 118[22] (cf. Mark 12[10-11] and Acts 4[11]).
See further Eph 2[20]. See also 1 Cor 10[4], '*and the rock was
Christ*'. Apparently the primitive Christian community used
testimonia, that is, collections of Messianic proof-texts, based
on this theme. Cf. Vincent Taylor, *The Names of Jesus*,
pp. 93–9. Paul means that the Jews stumbled at Christ, the
Stone of prophecy. That was why they did not seek righteousness by faith.

The first Christians, including Paul, did not read the Old
Testament as a modern student does, with the primary aim to
discover what the ancient writers actually meant. They used
the methods common to their time, but often with deep
religious insight.

10[1-2]. The deep emotion with which Paul contemplated the
stumbling of the Jews is reflected in **10[1-4]**. His heart's desire
and prayer to God is that they may be '*saved*', a term which,
as we have seen, has both present and future significance.
He bears them witness that they have '*a zeal for God*', but one
not based upon knowledge. Cf. Acts 17[23].

10[3-4]. Ignorant of God's way of putting men right with Himself, and seeking to establish their own way, they did not
submit themselves to God's way.

'*God's righteousness*' and '*the righteousness of God*' are used,
as in 1[17] and 3[21], of His action in accepting men as righteous
on the ground of their dependence upon Christ.

'*their own*' is a righteousness which consists in fulfilling
the Law.

'*they did not subject themselves*', that is, they did not respond
in faith and obedience.

'*For Christ is the end of the law unto righteousness*'. Cf.
Eph 2[15]. Most commentators think that the Mosaic Law is
meant, but some think that '*law*' means the legal principle, in
either case as the way to a right standing with God. The context supports the former interpretation. Christ is '*the end*'
in the sense that He terminates its validity as a way to righteousness. He is also '*the end*' because His teaching 'fulfils'

the law (12⁹; cf. Matt 5¹⁷), but this is not the idea in the present passage.

'*to everyone that believeth*', since by faith a man is justified.

10⁶. The principles of Law and Grace are now set in contrast.

First what Moses says in Lev 18⁵ is quoted (cf. Gal 3¹²), namely, that the man who practises the righteousness based on the Law shall obtain life thereby—an impossible way as Paul has shown (3²⁰, 7⁷⁻⁹).

10⁶⁻⁸. Secondly, the character of '*the righteousness which is of faith*' is described in phrases taken from Deut 30¹¹⁻¹⁴. What is there said about the Law is applied to Christ in a passage in which the new way of righteousness is personified. It is immediately available and is not dependent upon human striving. There is no need to seek it in heaven or in the abyss; it is near, in our mouth and in our heart.

Three times Paul adds the explanatory phrase, '*that is*'. No need to ascend, since Christ came to earth! No need to descend, since He is risen!; 'nigh', because present in the preached word!

10⁹⁻¹⁰. The conditions necessary for salvation are the outward confession of '*Jesus as Lord*' and the inward belief that He is risen. With the heart one believes and with the mouth confession is made, and the result is 'salvation' present and future. Although the language used has an individual reference ('*if thou*', verse 9), it reflects what was already happening in the earliest communities in baptism and public worship. It implies also the primitive creed, 'Jesus is Lord'. See the note on 1⁴.

For '*Jesus as Lord*' read 'Jesus is Lord'.

10¹¹. As often Paul supports his claim by an appeal to scripture, again quoting Isa 28¹⁶ (cf. 9³³) and adding 'every one' ('*whosoever*').

10¹²⁻¹³. As in 3²² he affirms that '*there is no distinction*', this time adding '*between Jew and Greek*', but whereas before he was thinking of sin, here the universality of the gospel is in question.

'*the same Lord*', he declares, '*is Lord of all, and is rich unto all that call upon him*', and he supports this affirmation by the words of Joel 2[32], '*Whosoever shall call upon the name of the Lord shall be saved*', applied by the prophet to the coming of '*the day of the Lord*'. It is interesting to see, and highly significant, that once the first Christians came to speak of Christ as Lord, they quoted passages from the Old Testament in which the name is that of God. Cf. Acts 2[21].

'*rich*'. Cf. Eph 3[8].

10[14-15]. '*How then shall they call on him in whom they have not believed? and how shall they believe in him whom they have not heard? and how shall they hear without a preacher? and how shall they preach, except they be sent?*' The purpose of these verses is not easy to determine. Is Paul describing a number of conditions which must be fulfilled if men are to call upon the name of the Lord? Or is he considering a number of pleas or excuses which the Jews might put forward in self-defence? Both considerations are relevant. The immediate intention is to lay down the conditions, but **10[16-21]** show that the interest is polemical.

To call upon the name of Christ, one must believe in Him. In order to believe, the good news must be heard; in order to hear it, the message must be preached; and in order to proclaim it, preachers must be sent. These are not new conditions; they are implicit in the words of the prophet, '*How beautiful are the feet of them that bring glad tidings of good things!*' (Isa 52[7]).

10[16-17]. These conditions were not fulfilled. '*Not all*' is an ironical understatement; Israel did not hearken. So manifest was the fact that scripture proof might seem unnecessary; but Paul's intention is to show that the failure was foreseen. Thus he quotes Isa 53[1]: '*Lord, who hath believed our report?*' Paul is quoting the passage in the sense in which it was understood in his day, and indeed until modern times. The meaning of the Hebrew is: 'Who could have believed that which we have heard?' (cf. *RV*m). The same passage is quoted in John 12[38].

Paul adds the comment: 'So faith comes of hearing, and hearing by gospel message.'

'*the word of Christ*' means the message about Christ.

10¹⁸. Paul himself now asks, '*Did they not hear?*' The form of the question conveys the meaning: 'You do not mean to say that they did *not* hear?' (J. Denney). A strong corrective follows.

'*Yea, verily*', or better, 'On the contrary' (C. F. D. Moule), introduces a quotation from Ps 19⁴. Cf. 1 Thess 1⁸, 2 Thess 3¹. There is no quotation formula, and Paul may be expressing in Scriptural language his claim that the gospel message has been proclaimed far and wide.

10¹⁹⁻²¹. A second question is now put: '*Did Israel not know?*' 'Surely you do not mean to say, then, *Israel did not understand?*' (J. Denney). In reply three Old Testament passages are quoted, and in accordance with current exegesis the author's name is mentioned.

The first quotation is from Deut 32²¹. The words '*provoke you to jealousy*' (cf. **11¹¹, ¹⁴**) and '*that which is no nation*' (cf. **9²⁵⁻⁶**) suggest that Paul has the Gentiles in mind, and the point (unstated) appears to be that if they could understand the message, Israel ought to have done so.

The second quotation is from Isa 65¹. When he says that Isaiah is 'very bold', he is emphasizing the prophet's courage.

'*that asked not of me*', that is, 'put no questions to me'. Again, Paul appears to have Gentiles in mind, although the passage refers to faithless Jews.

The third passage quoted is Isa 65². It is applied to Israel in the words, '*as to Israel*'. In the phrase, '*a disobedient and gainsaying people*', Paul finds the clue to the failure of Israel to understand the gospel message and to respond to it.

There might seem to be little in 9³⁰-10²¹ to engage the attention of a modern preacher, for the main theme, '*the righteousness of faith*', that is, the right standing with God which He makes possible through faith, is treated in earlier sections. There is, however, one outstanding subject which is suggested by Paul's analysis of the failure of the Jews, which can be applied to the situation of many people today, the inhibiting power of pride and rebellion against God which still makes faith impossible. 10¹⁴⁻¹⁵ is a passage rightly seen to be relevant to the work of Christian Missions, but, as in the case of many attractive New Testament texts, the original meaning must be considered first, that is, the conditions necessary for 'calling upon the Lord'.

(3) 11¹⁻³²: The Ultimate Purposes of God

In this section Paul takes up again the question of '*the remnant*', to which he had alluded in 9²⁷⁻⁹, and insists that it exists '*by grace*' and not on the basis of '*works*'. As foretold in scripture '*the rest were hardened*'. The idea that their fall was predetermined is rejected, but, it is argued, it was because of it that salvation has come to the Gentiles. Israel's loss is '*the riches of the Gentiles*'; '*how much more their fullness?*'

Meantime, it is urged, the Gentiles must not be '*highminded*'. A restoration of Israel is possible. The Gentiles are a wild olive grafted into the ancient stock; and why should not the broken branches of Israel be grafted back into their own olive? The '*hardening in part*' will persist '*until the fulness of the Gentiles be come in*'. All Israel shall yet be saved, as prophecy affirms, for God's gifts and call stand. '*God hath shut up all unto disobedience, that he might have mercy upon all*'.

11¹. Paul asks explicitly, '*Did God cast off his people?*' and emphatically replies, 'No' ('*God forbid*'). For him the thought is intolerable in view of his exalted Jewish descent. Cf. 2 Cor 11²², Phil 3⁵. As he says here, '*For I also am an Israelite, of the seed of Abraham, of the tribe of Benjamin*'. Cf. Phil 3⁵.

11²⁻⁵. With added emphasis the suggestion of God's repudiation of Israel is expressly rejected.

'*which he foreknew*' is no mere casual addition, but suggests a reason for the denial: God had full knowledge of the destiny of Israel.

An effective argument is now drawn from 1 Kings 19¹⁰, ¹⁴, ¹⁸.

'*of Elijah*', or literally, 'in Elijah', that is, in the part of scripture which tells his story.

'*how he pleadeth*', or 'accuses'.

The answer of God spoke of seven thousand men who had not bowed the knee to Baal, and Paul sees a parallel in the fact that at this present time there is a remnant of believing men.

'*Even so then at this present time also there is a remnant according to the election of grace*', that is, chosen and called by divine grace. Here Paul reverts to the ideas of Chapter **9**, but without raising those questions of freedom and responsibility which he has in mind all through Chapter **10**. He is manifestly anxious to repel any suggestions of merit which might be put forward on behalf of the remnant. This point he develops further in the next verse.

11⁶. If the calling is by grace, Paul says, '*it is no more of works*', a principle for which he has contended all through the Epistle. In saying, '*otherwise grace is no more grace*', he means that the rival principles are mutually self-exclusive.

11⁷. Paul sums up his argument thus far, but adds an important statement about 'hardening'. Israel did not obtain what she sought, but the Gentiles did.

'*the election*'. The abstract term is used instead of the concrete 'the elect', those called.

'*the rest were hardened*'. The Greek verb 'to harden' is formed from a word which means 'a stone' or 'callus', the hard substance at the end of a fractured bone. Cf. Mark 6⁵², 8¹⁷, 2 Cor 3¹⁴. Paul is thinking of a judicial hardening imposed upon persistently disobedient men. Cf. 1²⁴, ²⁶, ²⁸. Only so, like the prophets before him, can he explain to himself the facts of history. Cf. John 12³⁹⁻⁴⁰. Where we today should speak of a condition which is the natural consequence of sin, Jewish thinkers saw the act of God. The passages which follow in verses **8-10** show that Paul, or the first Christians if they had compiled a collection of *testimonia* ('testimonies'), had long reflected on the problem of Israel's failure.

11⁸⁻¹⁰. The first quotation is based on Deut 29⁴ and Isa 29¹⁰ (cf. also Isa 6⁹⁻¹⁰).

'*a spirit of stupor*', that is insensibility to spiritual values so that they should neither see nor hear.

'*unto this very day*'. Cf. Acts 7⁵¹.

The second quotation is from Ps 69²²⁻³, here assigned to David. It is used, without regard to its original meaning, as a description of the Jews mainly because of the word '*stumbling-block*'. The Greek word was used of the bait-stick in a trap, but 'pitfall' (Moffatt, *RSV*) is a better rendering.

11¹¹. '*Did they stumble that they might fall?*' Very many commentators render the second clause 'so as to fall', a translation which is grammatically possible. But since Paul answers the question with an indignant 'No' ('*God forbid*'), it is more probable that the clause is a 'purpose-clause': was the fall God's ultimate purpose?

Paul points out, however, that in the order of God's providence, by Israel's stumbling, salvation came to the Gentiles.

'*their fall*'. The word used commonly means 'trespass', but the basic meaning of the word, 'false step', seems more appropriate.

'*for to provoke them to jealousy*'. This idea first appears in 10[19] in the quotation from Deut 32[21]. Paul uses it here to suggest a further purpose in the stumbling. Was it meant, through the spectacle of the triumphant Gentile Mission, to bring the Jews to a better mind, to desire, in short, what the Gentiles had obtained?

11[12]. '*Now if their fall is the riches of the world, and their loss the riches of the Gentiles; how much more their fulness?*' The false step has had beneficent results, namely the world's enrichment, and the impoverishing of Israel has brought wealth to the Gentiles. What, then, if they are brought to full strength? Already in this obscure passage Paul's interpretation of Israel's fall begins to appear.

'*their loss*'. The word used is difficult to translate, as the renderings of modern translators show: 'failure' (*RSV*), 'defeat' (Goodspeed, Sanday and Headlam), 'defection' (Moffatt).

'*their fulness*'. An equally difficult word: 'full inclusion' (*RSV*), 'complement' (Sanday and Headlam). J. Armitage Robinson, *St Paul's Epistle to the Ephesians*, p. 259, has shown that the Greek word can be used of the cargo or the crew of a ship. It is remarkable that, however difficult translation may be, Paul's general meaning is clear. Doubtless this is because he returns to the same thought in verse 15.

11[13-14]. '*to you that are Gentiles*'. Better, 'to you Gentiles'. The phrase indicates that the Church at Rome consisted mainly of Gentiles.

Paul suggests that, while he magnifies his ministry to the Gentiles, another motive impels him. So far from despising his fellow countrymen, he wants to make them jealous and save some of them. He wants to glorify his ministry as '*an apostle of Gentiles*' in order to help to bring about the conversion of his fellow-countrymen by provoking them to envy the Gentiles. This, of course, was not Paul's primary Apostolic purpose, and it looks very much like a reply of his to Jewish criticisms.

'*them that are my flesh*'. The Greek has nothing corresponding to '*them that are*' but simply '*my flesh*', a phrase which
strongly expresses his unity with them.

'*if by any means*'. Cf. 1¹⁰. The phrase suggests an objective
earnestly considered.

'*some of them*'. This phrase may bear on the interpretation
of 'all Israel' in verse 26.

11¹⁵. The verse repeats the ideas of verse 12, but with greater
clarity. If the result of the rejection ('*casting away*') of the
Jews is a reconciliation on a world-wide scale, what will the
receiving of them mean?

Paul answers his question by the words '*life from the dead*',
that is, spiritual resurrection, in the consummation of the
Kingdom of God. This hope is based on considerations
mentioned in the next verse.

11¹⁶. '*If the firstfruit is holy, so is the lump*'. The imagery is
explained by the reference to the heave offering in Num 15¹⁹⁻²¹.
In accordance with ancient ideas of sacrifice the offering of the
firstfruits was believed to carry with it the consecration of the
whole. By the '*firstfruit*' Paul is thinking of Abraham, Isaac,
and Jacob, and he believes that their holiness consecrates the
Jewish people in the sense of setting them apart (which is the
root idea of Old Testament holiness) for the fulfilment of
God's purposes. In short, they must have a future. This idea
of racial solidarity meant more to the ancient world than it
does to us, although for us, too, it is meaningful.

'*If the root is holy, so are the branches*'. The same idea is
expressed in the imagery of a tree.

If pressed unduly this principle would be in conflict with
the claim that not all Abraham's seed are children of God,
but with due regard to the facts of freedom and responsibility
it is valid. The heritage of one's nation, school, family, and
home is incalculable.

11¹⁷⁻²⁴. In this section the illustration of the olive tree is
developed. For the use of the image in the prophets see
Jer 11¹⁶ and Hos 14⁶, and for the parallel figure of the vine see
Isa 5⁷, Ps 80⁸, and John 15¹⁻⁵. It is often said that Paul was
no horticulturalist, for wild olive branches are not grafted into
a cultivated stock, nor broken branches from the latter grafted

back into their own olive. Sanday and Headlam, however, point out that Paul's argument depends upon the process being an unnatural one; cf. *The Epistle to the Romans*, p. 328. Is this what Paul meant? Cf. F. J. Leenhardt, 'Paul may even have realized that he was suggesting a not quite natural process', *The Epistle to the Romans*, p. 288.

11¹⁷. '*some*'. An intentional understatement.

'*and thou, being a wild olive, wast grafted in among them*'. The phrase continues the description of the unnatural process of the ingrafting of the Gentiles into the stock of Israel.

'*partaker with them of the root of the fatness of the olive tree*'. It is a cardinal principle of Paul's theology that the Church is the New Israel and therefore shares in the blessings of the Old Testament covenants.

The whole verse is a conditional sentence of the type, 'If these things are so, what then?' Verse **18** is the answer.

11¹⁸⁻²⁰. It is noteworthy that the major portion of the section is devoted to a warning to the Gentiles. They are not to boast over the branches, for it is not they who support the root, but the root them.

'*Thou wilt say then*'. Perhaps Paul knew of Gentile Christians who despised the Jews. And they are still to be found. The passage rebukes anti-Semitism. Unbelief caused the branches to be broken off and the Christian stands only in virtue of his faith.

'*Be not highminded, but fear*' does not commend a craven fear, but a constant sense of awe at the goodness of God.

11²¹⁻². '*For if God spared not the natural branches, neither will he spare thee. Behold then the goodness and severity of God*'. Presumption is folly. Paul does not hesitate to speak of the '*severity*' as well as of '*the goodness of God*'. Far indeed is he from the easy belief, 'He's a Good Fellow, and 'twill all be well' (*The Rubá'iyát*, lxiv).

'*if thou continue in his goodness*', that is, by faith moment by moment. '*Otherwise*', Paul adds, '*thou also shalt be cut off*'.

11²³⁻⁴. The figure is now used to suggest the possibility of the restoration of Israel.

'*if they continue not in their unbelief*'. This is the essential condition.

'*contrary to nature*'. Paul is not quite blind to the strangeness of his illustration.

Surely, Paul argues, God will graft back '*the natural branches*' into '*their own olive tree*'.

11²⁵⁻⁷. What has been suggested is now affirmed.

'*I would not . . . have you ignorant*'. Cf. **1¹³**, 1 Cor 10¹, 12¹, 2 Cor 1⁸, 1 Thess 4³.

'*this mystery*'. The use of the term may have been suggested by the pagan mystery-religions, but it is used with the difference that for Paul the mystery is an open secret. The mystery mentioned here is that '*a hardening in part hath befallen Israel*'.

'*a hardening in part*'. Cf. **11⁵, ⁷, ¹⁷**. As in the case of Pharaoh (**9¹⁷**) the hardening is conceived as a judgement imposed by God.

'*until the fulness of the Gentiles be come in*'. The hardening is temporary as well as partial. A limit is set. Cf. Luke 21²⁴, '*until the times of the Gentiles be fulfilled*'. '*the fulness*' (cf. verse **12**) is the complement, the completed number.

'*and so all Israel shall be saved*'. This statement hardly amounts to universalism. Paul is thinking of Israel as a whole, and not necessarily of every individual Israelite.

'*as it is written*' is Paul's usual formula of citation. He quotes Isa 59²⁰⁻¹ with the addition in 27*b* of a phrase from Isa 27⁹. By '*the Deliverer*' Paul understands Christ the Messiah, and it is of interest to note that Isa 59²⁰ is interpreted Messianically in the Babylonian *Talmud* (cf. J. Knox, *The Epistle to the Romans, The Interpreter's Bible*, IX.575). The promise that He shall turn away ungodliness from Jacob is characterized by the prophet as '*my covenant unto them*'. By the use of Isa 27⁹ it is related by Paul to the taking away of sins.

11²⁸⁻⁹. The situation is summed up from the two standpoints of the gospel and the election purpose of God. In the light of the former the Jews are '*enemies*' of God, but from the standpoint of the latter they are '*beloved for the fathers' sake*'. The reference is to the Patriarchs and the claim in verse **16**. Paul's confidence is based on the unchangeable purpose of God.

'*The gifts*', he declares, '*and the calling of God are without repentance*', that is, they are irrevocable.

11³⁰⁻¹. There is a parallel, he holds, between the situation of the Gentiles and the Jews, fulfilled in the one case, to be fulfilled in the other. By the disobedience of the Jews the Gentiles have '*obtained mercy*', and by the mercy shown to the Gentiles the Jews will also '*obtain mercy*', being provoked, presumably, to seek it. Such appears to be Paul's argument.

11³². '*For God hath shut up all unto disobedience, that he might have mercy upon all*'. An epigram clinches the argument which bears upon the whole problem of sin. It should be treated as an epigram and not as a formal proposition. God, he claims, has shut together all men in situations which issue in disobedience, but His ultimate purpose is not malevolence, but mercy for all. He desires men, not morons. A similar thought appears in Gal 3²²: 'Howbeit the scripture hath shut up all things under sin, that the promise by faith in Jesus Christ might be given to them that believed.' In the present passage, in saying that '*God hath shut up all unto disobedience, that he might have mercy upon all*', qualifications, generally left to be supplied in an epigram, are not mentioned. If challenged Paul would have denied that disobedience is inevitable and mercy automatic. His repeated emphasis on unbelief and faith shows this. For similar reasons we may doubt if '*all*' means every individual. He is thinking of groups throughout the chapter.

To anyone who makes a close study of the chapter it must seem strange that preachers can be satisfied to choose peripheral subjects when striking texts introducing foundation Christian principles are available. Nothing can be more mistaken than to suppose that Paul's teaching is out of date or even out of touch with the problems of modern life. The following texts have each a timely and timeless significance: '*But if it is by grace, it is no more of works: otherwise grace is no more grace*' (11⁶); '*if the firstfruit is holy, so is the lump: and if the root is holy, so are the branches*' (11¹⁶); '*it is not thou that bearest the root, but the root thee*' (11¹⁸); '*Be not highminded, but fear*' (11²⁰); '*The gifts and the calling of God are without repentance*' (11²⁹); and, if a preacher has enough courage, '*God hath shut up all unto disobedience, that he might have mercy upon all*' (11³²). In each case study kindles the text, exposition makes it lucid, and insight shows its relevance. Only if it first burns in the mind is it likely to warm the heart, but it is tinder to the flame.

11[33-6]: Paul's Sense of Awe as He contemplates the Ways of God

It is characteristic of Paul that, although he has been grappling with a human problem in the field of history, he ends with a cry of wonder as he thinks of the eternal purpose of God.

11[33]. '*O the depth of the riches both of the wisdom and the knowledge of God!*' It seems better with the *RV*m to read 'of the riches and the wisdom and the knowledge', the riches being those of His grace (cf. Sanday and Headlam, *The Epistle to the Romans*, p. 339).

'*unsearchable*' in the sense that they cannot be exhausted.

'*past tracing out*'. The Schoolmen of the Middle Ages said: 'All things go out in mystery.'

11[34]. '*For who hath known the mind of the Lord? or who hath been his counsellor?*' The quotation is from Isa 40[13]. Cf. also 1 Cor 2[16]. Like the unknown prophet of the Exile Paul is thrilled by the thought of the utter sufficiency of God.

11[35]. The second quotation is from Job 41[11]. Cf. Acts 17[25]. Paul uses the passage to suggest that so rich are the riches of God that no one can impart anything to Him. He is no man's debtor.

11[36]. In a magnificent passage we are left with the thought of God as the source, medium, sustainer, and end of all things, and a benediction closes the long section. Cf. 1 Cor 8[6].

FOUR

Life in the New Age Made Possible

12¹-15¹³. This fourth part of the Epistle is hortatory and 'practical'. It is closely linked in thought with all that has been set forth in Chapters **1-11.** It describes the life of the justified man in the complex relationships of human society. Various aspects of the new life are described in sections which may conveniently be distinguished as follows: (1) **12¹⁻²¹**, Life within the Christian community; (2) **13¹⁻¹⁴**, The Life of the Community in its Outward Relationships; (3) **14¹-15¹³**, The Strong and the Weak in Communal Life. The overriding theme of the whole is Christian Love.

(1) 12¹⁻²¹: Life within the Christian Community

It would be mistaken to separate this section and 13¹⁻¹⁴ too sharply but the reference to '*one body in Christ*' seems to suggest that in **12¹⁻²¹** Paul has for the most part in mind relationships between individuals within the Christian community. Various forms of ministration are mentioned and exhortations bearing upon personal relationships are given.

12¹. '*therefore*' points back to the doctrinal exposition as a whole, and '*by the mercies of God*' recalls the emphasis on mercy in **11³⁰⁻²**.

'*present your bodies*'. The idea of presenting an offering often occurs in sacrificial contexts. This is one of the places in which the rendering '*bodies*' is too narrow an interpretation; 'your own selves' is a better translation. So Barrett, 'the whole human person'; also J. Knox, and others.

'*a living sacrifice*' marks a contrast to the slain sacrifices of the Temple ritual. The offering is described as '*holy*', that is, consecrated to God, and as '*acceptable*' or 'well pleasing' to Him. Cf. Heb 13¹⁵.

'*which is your reasonable service*'. The word translated '*service*' is frequently used of 'worship', and 'spiritual' (cf.

1 Pet 2²) is to be preferred to '*reasonable*'. The offering of ourselves to God is 'spiritual worship'. *NEB*, 'the worship offered by mind and heart'.

12². '*be not fashioned according to this world*'. The Jewish contrast between '*this age*' and '*that which is to come*' must be remembered in reading this passage. Cf. Matt 12³², Luke 20³⁴ᶠ, Eph 1²¹, Heb 6⁵. 'This age' is regarded as fleeting, and already by faith the Christian is a citizen of 'the Age to Come'. Cf. Phil 3²⁰, '*For our citizenship is in heaven.*' To allow ourselves, therefore, to be shaped according to the ideas and standards of the present world is disloyalty and is destructive of our true citizenship.

'*but be ye transformed*'. The verb used is that which appears in the story of the Transfiguration (Mark 9³), but here the transformation is inward.

'*by the renewing of your mind*'. Cf. 1 Pet 1¹⁴. For Paul's use of the term '*mind*', the inner self, see the notes on 7²³, ²⁵. The renewing is especially the work of the Holy Spirit.

'*that ye may prove*', that is, 'discern', but the verb can also mean 'to approve'. See 2¹⁸, Phil 1¹⁰. What is to be discerned is the '*will of God*' characterized as '*good, acceptable* (or 'well-pleasing', *RV*m), *and perfect*'.

12³. This verse recalls what Paul has already said in **11²⁰**, '*Be not highminded, but fear*'.

'*through the grace that was given me*'. There is a note of divine authority in the words; Paul is not merely expressing an opinion.

The warning is against conceit, always a danger in a community.

'*but so to think as to think soberly*', that is, to think in a way which results in sober-mindedness, a Greek virtue commended by Aristotle.

'*according as God hath dealt to each man a measure of faith*'. This principle for thinking means that faith itself is a means of insight, that it is given to us and is not of our creating, and that as yet it exists in part. Cf. **1¹⁷**, '*by faith unto faith*'.

Dependence on God begets humility.

12⁴⁻⁵. The idea of the community as 'the Body of Christ' is introduced here (from 1 Cor 12¹²⁻³¹) because the qualities commended, modesty, sober-mindedness, and discernment of the will of God, are social in their implications. Cf. also Eph 4[15], Col 1[18].

'*in one body*'. The figure is that of the physical body and its members, but a moral relationship is described. For the fuller development of the figure see 1 Cor 12[12-31].

'*one body in Christ*'. Elsewhere Paul speaks of Christ as '*the Head of the Body*'; cf. Col 1[18], also Col 2[19], Eph 1[22-3], 4[15], and 5[23]. See also Col 1[24], 3[5], and Eph 2[16]. Cf. *The Names of Jesus*, pp. 100–3. We are '*members one of another*' because we share a common life centred in Christ.

12[6-8]. The ideas of this passage are clear, but the text offers difficulties. In the *RV* the phrases '*let us prophesy*', '*let us give ourselves*', '*let him do it*' are printed in italics because they are understood in order to give meaning to the ellipses in the Greek text. Many commentators read the passage in this way. The alternative is to put a comma after verse 5, or to read 'We have' instead of 'having'. 'But we have grace-gifts which differ according to the grace that was given us, whether that of prophecy (differing) according to the measure of our faith, or that of service (differing) in the sphere of the service, or he that teaches (exercising his gift) in his teaching, or he that exhorts in his exhorting, he who gives (exercising this charism) in singleness of purpose, he who holds office in a deep sense of responsibility, he who shows compassion in cheerfulness' (J. H. Moulton, *A Grammar of New Testament Greek*, I.183).

'*prophecy*', inspired preaching.

'*according to the proportion of our faith*'. The faith mentioned is personal faith, not 'the faith' or Christian confession. A significant qualification for preachers.

'*ministry*'. Probably attendance upon the practical needs of fellow Christians is meant.

'*he that teacheth*'. Catechists appear to be meant. The need for them must have been felt from the earliest days.

'*he that exhorteth*'. Another aspect of the preacher's office.

'*liberality*'. The word used also means 'simplicity'.

'*he that ruleth*', that is, the man who exercises oversight in the community and in the family in the way of administration. Cf. 1 Thess 5[12], 1 Tim 5[17], and also 1 Tim 3[4-5, 12].

'*he that sheweth mercy*', in deeds of mercy. The spirit in

which acts of kindness are done ('*cheerfulness*') is as important as the deed.

12⁹⁻¹³. A series of injunctions follows. Love is to be unfeigned. The readers are to abhor evil and to cleave to that which is good. '*In love of the brethren*', that is, toward all the members of the community, they are to be warmly affectionate one to another, surpassing one another in showing honour. Unflagging in zeal, they are to be fervent in spirit, serving the Lord, to rejoice in hope, to be resolute in persecution, constant in prayer. They are to contribute to the needs of others and to pursue the practice of hospitality. The duty of hospitality was highly esteemed in the early Church.

12¹⁴⁻¹⁵. '*Bless them that persecute you*'. Paul seems to have in mind the saying of Jesus, '*But I say unto you, Love your enemies, and pray for them that persecute you*' (Matt 5⁴⁴, Luke 6²⁷⁻⁸). Paul is thinking of the relationships between the community and those outside, but that he has the community mainly in mind, is shown by his exhortation to the readers to share one another's joys and sorrows.

12¹⁶. '*Be of the same mind*'. Cf. 15⁵, 2 Cor 13⁵, Phil 2², and 4². The counsel does not mean that they are to think alike, but that they are to be harmonious in their common relationships.

'*Set not your mind on high things*'. Cf. **11²⁰, 12³.**

'*but condescend to things that are lowly*'. The verb used suggests the idea of accommodating oneself to things or persons. The *RSV* and Moffatt have 'associate with' and both think that persons are meant; 'humble folk', 'the lowly'. This rendering may be correct, but '*high things*' suggests that '*things that are lowly*' are meant.

'*Be not wise in your own conceits*' appears to be drawn from Prov 3⁷. *RSV* and Moffatt, 'Never be conceited'.

12¹⁷⁻¹⁸. '*Render to no man evil for evil*'. Cf. Matt 5³⁹, ⁴³⁻⁴.

'*Take thought for things honourable in the sight of all men*' is an adaptation of Prov 3⁴. Cf. 2 Cor 4², 8²¹.

'*as much as in you lieth*', that is, as far as you are concerned.

'*Be at peace with all men*'. Cf. Mark 9⁵⁰, '*Be at peace one with another*'.

12¹⁹⁻²¹. '*wrath*'. Probably God's wrath is meant. Cf. **1¹⁸, 3⁵, 9²²**. The quotation is from Deut 32³⁵.

'*if thine enemy hunger*'. Again Paul is quoting the Book of Proverbs; see Prov 25²¹⁻².

'*coals of fire*'. The phrase is commonly explained as meaning 'the burning pangs of shame'. Leenhardt, 'the pain of repentance acting like an inner fire burning the conscience'.

Paul sums up his counsel in the sentence: '*Be not overcome of evil, but overcome evil with good.*'

Almost every verse in this chapter offers subjects for preaching, especially verse 1 (The Self as a Living Sacrifice) and verse 2 (The Renewing of the Mind). It is of essential importance to observe these counsels are not detached moral exhortations, but are injunctions arising out of all that Paul has said about the Righteousness of God and His purposes for Jew and Gentile.

(2) 13¹⁻¹⁴: The Life of the Community in its Outward Relationships

In this section Paul discusses the question of obedience to civil authorities **13¹⁻⁷**, love as the fulfilment of the Law, and the moral urgency of the End Time. Paul, it is to be noted, is far more interested in the ethical demands of the End in relation to the present than in its details and does not mention here the Parousia or coming of Christ.

13¹. '*every soul*', that is, every person. The expression is Hebraic.

'*be in subjection to*', or '*be subject to*'.

'*the higher powers*'. This abstract expression denotes 'those in authority', the civil rulers.

'*for there is no power but of God*'. Paul adds '*and the powers that be are ordained of God*'. He is manifestly thinking of Imperial Rome which gave unity to the world of his day, established law and order, put down piracy, and gave protection to travellers like himself. As yet, it must be remembered, Rome had not persecuted Christians, although the fact that Christianity was not a religion recognized by law must have warned the Apostle of perils to come; cf. **8³⁵⁻⁸**. There is at the same time a Jewish strain in Paul's teaching, in his emphasis upon the sovereignty of God and his belief that authority is delegated by Him to rulers and kings. For similar teaching see 1 Pet 2¹³⁻¹⁷ and 1 Tim 2¹⁻².

13². This verse brings out the consequences of Paul's position. To resist the civil power is to withstand God's ordinance and to expose oneself to His judgement. He may be thinking of Jewish fanatics. Ten years later the Zealots were largely responsible for the horrors of the siege of Jerusalem.

If taken at its face value, this teaching can be used to defend civil obedience under tyranny, as taught in the earlier Tudor period during the reign of Charles the First and under Communist and Fascist rule. Paul, however, does not raise the question what is to be done when rulers are bad and tyrannical. For a different attitude to Rome, as a persecuting power, see Rev 18.

13³⁻⁴. '*rulers*', Paul can say, '*are not a terror to the good work, but to the evil*'. The good man, he holds, has nothing to fear.

'*the good work*'. By a minute change of the Greek text it has been suggested that Paul wrote 'the good man'. Cf. Moffatt, 'an honest man'.

The references to '*wrath*' (verse **4**) and '*the wrath*' (verse **5**) are, as in **12¹⁹**, to God's judgement. If so, we must infer that Paul thinks of the ruler's power to punish as a delegated authority, of which '*the sword*' is the symbol.

13⁵. A higher motive than fear is introduced in the phrase '*for conscience sake*'. See the notes on **2¹⁵** and **9¹**. For a valuable discussion of the whole question of the Christian's attitude to the State, see P. S. Watson, *The State as a Servant of God* (1946).

13⁶⁻⁷. The same motive justifies the payment of taxes. Paul may well have in mind the saying of Jesus: 'Render unto Cæsar the things that are Cæsar's, and unto God the things that are God's' (Mark 12¹⁷).

'*tribute*', the Imperial dues.

'*custom*', better 'taxes' or 'revenue'.

'*fear*' in this context has the meaning of 'respect'.

13⁸⁻¹⁰. From the question of civil dues Paul turns to the love which is owed to everyone. It is the one debt that cannot fully be discharged. The injunction, '*Owe no man anything, save to love one another*', is one of his finest utterances. Cf. John 13³⁴, Jas 2⁸.

'*he that loveth his neighbour hath fulfilled the law*'. Since the commandments are cited, it is probable that '*the law*' is the Mosaic Law. Some of the best Jewish teachers taught the same truth. Paul is probably familiar with the teaching of Jesus concerning the great commandment (Mark 12²⁸⁻³⁴), and, like Jesus, quotes Lev 19¹⁸, '*Thou shalt love thy neighbour as thyself*'.

'*summed up*'. Cf. Eph 1¹⁰.

'*the fulfilment*'. That which fills it up or completes it.

13¹¹. Paul now enforces his exhortations by a reference to the approach of the End.

'*the season*', that is, the appointed time. Cf. Mark 1¹⁵, 1 Cor 7²⁹, Heb 9⁹.

'*to awake out of sleep*'. The same imagery is used in 1 Thess 5⁶, 1 Cor 15³⁴, and Eph 5¹⁴. Literally rendered, the passage runs: 'It is already the hour to arise out of sleep.' Cf. Matt 25⁶.

'*salvation*'. The passage clearly illustrates the eschatological significance which salvation has for Paul. Present and future in character, it is here used of complete and final deliverance from sin and death. It is '*nearer*' than when the first response of faith was made.

13¹². '*The night is far spent, and the day is at hand*'. The first Christians lived in the belief that the Day of the Lord was near. See 1 Thess 4¹⁵⁻¹⁸, 5¹⁻¹¹. This belief was based on the teaching of Jesus (cf. Luke 17²²⁻³⁷, Mark 9¹, 13³⁰⁻¹), although Jesus Himself said that He did not know the day or the hour (Mark 13³²). A change of view can be traced in the thought of Paul. In 1 Thessalonians he expects the Parousia during his life time (4¹⁵) and in 1 Corinthians he believes that it is very near (cf. 7²⁹⁻³¹), so much so that family arrangements are of second importance, but in later letters he does not expect personally to live to see it. Cf. 2 Cor 5¹⁻¹⁰, Phil 1²³. But he never renounces his expectation of the coming of '*the Day*' (cf. Phil 1⁶, ¹⁰, 2¹⁶, 3²⁰). In the present section, the only allusion of its kind in the Epistle, all the emphasis lies on the moral urgency of the hope.

For us today, after an interval of more than nineteen centuries, the expectation of the Coming of Christ is less easy to hold, and it is often left to the speculations of strange sects. But it is improbable that the present world order can continue indefinitely, and a sense of tension belongs to the Christian experience. But when, and in what way, the consummation will come it is impossible to say and presumptuous to attempt to foretell. Meantime Paul's exhortations are always timely. We are to cast off '*the works of darkness*' and put on '*the armour of light*'.

For other references to the Christian armour, a favourite figure of Paul, see **6¹³**, 1 Thess 5⁸, 2 Cor 6⁷, Eph 6¹¹⁻¹⁷.

13¹³. '*Let us walk honestly, as in the day*', that is, as though it had already dawned. Paul uses the Old Testament metaphor of walking to denote Christian conduct more frequently than any other New Testament writer. He also frequently stresses the idea of seemliness.

'*honestly*'. The word used means 'decorously', 'becomingly'. Cf. 1 Thess 4¹², 1 Cor 14¹⁰. Paul has a strong sense of the importance of what is fitting.

The passage which follows about renouncing revelling, drunkenness, unlawful intercourse, and wanton vice is the one on which the eye of Augustine lighted when he heard the child sing 'Take and read; take and read'. 'I neither wished nor needed to read further,' Augustine writes. 'With the end of that sentence, as though the light of assurance had poured into my heart, all the shades of doubt were scattered. I put my finger in the page and closed the book; I turned to Alypius with a calm countenance, and told him' (*Confessions*, viii.12).

13¹⁴. '*put ye on the Lord Jesus Christ*'. Cf. Gal 3²⁷. The figure of clothing is used of righteousness in Job 29¹⁴ and Ps 132⁹, of power in Luke 24⁴⁹, and of the new man in Eph 4²⁴ and Col 3¹⁰.

'*and make not provision*'. The Greek word is used of 'forethought' or 'care' here and in Acts 23³.

'*flesh*'. This is one of the cases in which the word is used of human nature dominated by sin. See the note on 7¹⁴.

'*to fulfil the lusts thereof*'. The Greek is 'unto lusts' or 'unto its lusts', that is, with a view to them or in order to satisfy them. The '*lusts*' are evil desires. See 1[24]. The two counsels are not merely co-ordinate. Where Christ is 'put on' evil forethought is not exercised.

Apart from 13[8], '*Owe no man anything, save to love one another*', which commends honesty, but reminds us of our perpetual insolvency, the chapter serves to remind the preacher of neglected themes. Our duty to the State is one of these, and yet it has special interest today in the face of world problems. We perilously neglect the End and the Coming of Christ. To treat these themes is difficult, since we cannot remain silent about the delay of the Parousia and all the problems it raises. Yet these are days of Crisis in which Paul's injunctions have lost none of their urgency. Modern psychology at its best has not a little to say concerning the ideas which lie behind the injunction to be clothed with Christ and so not to plan for evil desires.

(3) 14[1]-15[13]: The Strong and the Weak in Communal Life

In this section Paul deals with practical questions of conduct concerning the eating of meats and the observance of holy days which he had encountered at Corinth and in other communities. It has been suggested that he has in mind a definite sect or party in the Church at Rome consisting of ascetics who abstained from meat and wine, but this suggestion is unnecessary and is not supported by the character of the Epistle as a whole. It seems better to suppose that Paul is drawing upon his own past experience. In his view the scruples he mentions are of no importance in themselves, but they are to be respected by those to whom they are matters of indifference since by their attitude or practice the conscience of others may be injured. It is noteworthy that he does not put forward merely prudential considerations, but makes everything turn upon faith and love, upon the example of Christ Himself who '*pleased not himself*' (15[3]), and upon the fact that our final allegiance is to Him. In the last six verses he sums up much for which he has contended in the Epistle.

14[1]. '*him that is weak in faith*'. The weakness is one of judgement arising out of a feeble grasp of the implications of righteousness by faith. Cf. 15[1], 1 Cor 8[9].
　'*receive ye*', that is, into Christian fellowship.

'yet not to doubtful disputations'. The *RSV* rendering, 'not for disputes over opinions', is better. So too *NEB*, 'without attempting to settle doubtful points'.

14²⁻³. The question of food is cited as a case in point.

'herbs'. Vegetables are meant.

'set at nought', that is 'despise'. The opposite attitude (*'judge'*) is fault-finding, censoriousness. The reason given is the need for charity toward him whom God has received.

14⁴. Still addressing the weak, Paul reminds them that the person judged is God's household servant, and that to Him he must give account. God, moreover, will look after him!

14⁵. A second case of scruple is that of the observance of holy days. Probably the issue is that of observing the Jewish Sabbath.

'mind'. See the note on 7²⁵. 'In his own judgement' is meant. He is to be fully convinced.

14⁶⁻⁸. Paul points out that, however different the conclusions reached may be, each man has the same aim, to be well-pleasing to God, for the believer lives and dies in obedience to his Lord. True as it may be that no man lives or dies to himself in view of his social relationships, it is not this idea which Paul expresses in verse **7**, but that of the Christian's relationship to God. It is difficult to be certain whether in this section Paul is thinking of God or of Christ, but verse **9** suggests that in verse **8** Christ is meant.

14⁹. *'died, and lived again'*. The reference is to Christ's death and resurrection. Here Paul affirms that the purpose of both is Christ's lordship. Cf. Phil 2⁹⁻¹¹.

14¹⁰⁻¹². A further argument is now advanced, the fact that we shall stand before the judgement-seat of God, a truth of which he finds an illustration in Isa 45²³. Cf. 2 Cor 5¹⁰.

'confess', that is, 'acknowledge', or 'praise'. Cf. Phil 2⁹⁻¹¹. The solemnity which the thought of the Last Judgement has for Paul is powerfully expressed in 1 Cor 4³⁻⁴.

14¹³⁻¹⁴. Playing on the word '*judge*', Paul insists that the main point to consider is the peril of putting a stumbling-block in someone else's way. He is fully convinced, or, as he puts it, '*persuaded in the Lord Jesus*', that nothing is impure in itself, yet in the mind of him who thinks it so, it is impure. Here Paul is addressing the strong.

14¹⁵⁻¹⁶. It is a shrewd thrust when he says: '*Destroy not with thy meat him for whom Christ died.*' Yet he cannot mean that vegetarianism is a Christian duty. Evidently a principle is being invoked here which cannot be of universal application, but has to be adjudged in each individual case in accordance with the maxim: '*Let not your good be evil spoken of.*'

14¹⁷⁻¹⁸. Eating and drinking, it is implied, are not matters of importance so far as '*the kingdom of God*' is concerned. The Kingdom is God's kingly rule which is present already and is to be consummated hereafter. Under this rule the really significant things are '*righteousness and peace and joy in the Holy Ghost*'. Here '*righteousness*' is right doing, '*peace*' is the condition which should obtain within the community, and '*joy*' through the Spirit should be the experience of all. Paul does not speak of the Kingdom often (12 times), but his teaching, particularly here, is in full harmony with that of Christ.

'*herein*' (in verse **18**) refers to the three qualities just mentioned.

'*approved*'. The word was used of the testing of metals. Cf. **16¹⁰**. It should be noted that while Paul puts first the idea of being '*well-pleasing to God*', he values the approval of men based upon testing.

14¹⁹⁻²¹. Exhortations follow. Believers are to pursue things that make for peace and mutual upbuilding. Cf. 1 Cor 14²⁶, 1 Thess 5¹¹. They are not to throw down the work of God for meat's sake. While all things are clean, the man who eats in a way which causes others to stumble is in the wrong. The good thing is not to eat meat and not to drink wine, nor indeed to do anything which causes a brother's fall.

14²². '*The faith which thou hast, have thou to thyself before God*'. that is, let it be between God and yourself, do not use it to fix standards for others. Happy, thinks Paul, is the man who does not pass sentence upon himself by what he approves.

14²³. Very different is the case of the man who eats with doubts in his mind. He is condemned because his action is not guided by his faith.

'*and whatsoever is not of faith is sin*'. In this final aphorism Paul sums up his discussion. '*Not of faith*' does not mean 'what is not determined by correct teaching', but 'that which is not in harmony with our dependence upon God', faith in the personal sense of the word. Anything which is in conflict with that faith, disturbing or destroying it, is sin because it is self-regarding action. The point is that living faith is the touchstone which tests conduct and shows the right way.

15¹⁻³. There is no break between the chapters. Paul now addresses the '*strong*' directly. The counsel '*to bear the infirmities of the weak*', and '*not to please ourselves*', is based on the example of Christ who '*pleased not himself*'. Again, as in **14¹⁹**, the end in view is the upbuilding of others. The language of Ps 69⁹, '*The reproaches of them that reproached thee fell upon me*', is put into the lips of Christ: He bore reproaches addressed to God.

15⁴. Paul takes occasion to justify the use of the Old Testament, claiming that the counsels in it '*were written for our learning*' (that is, instruction) in order that we might have '*hope*'. This hope is not hope in general, but confidence in the fulfilment of God's purposes.

'*patience*'. Better, 'endurance'. See the note on **5³⁻⁴**.

'*comfort*'. We should probably read 'exhortation' or 'encouragement' (*RSV*).

15⁵⁻⁷. '*The God of patience and of comfort*'. Read 'of endurance and encouragement'. The words are a prayer for unity.

'*to be of the same mind*'. See the note on **12¹⁶**. The standard of agreement is described in the phrase, '*according to Christ Jesus*'. The purpose is to glorify God, '*the God and Father of our Lord Jesus Christ*'. The result is to be seen in welcoming one another, as Christ welcomed them, and all '*to the glory of God*'.

15[8-12]. The remaining verses of the section are more closely related to **5-7** than would appear at first sight. Paul is concerned to speak of Jew and Gentile not only to repeat leading ideas in the Epistle, but in order to strengthen the exhortation to accept one another as Christ accepted them, the strong and the weak, to the glory of God.

'*a minister of the circumcision*', that is, a servant of the Jews.

'*for the truth of God*', that is, to maintain it, and this, by confirming the promises given to the fathers.

'*the fathers*', the Jewish patriarchs; cf. **4**[16], **9**[5].

'*and that the Gentiles might glorify God for his mercy*'. This is a second and parallel reason for Christ's humiliation (He was '*a servant.*'). The Gentiles are included in the promises made to the fathers. Old Testament passages are added to show this: Ps 18[49], Deut 32[43], Ps 117[1], and Isa 11[20]. These quotations show how deeply Paul had pondered over the scriptures to justify his mission to the Gentiles.

15[13]. '*Now the God of hope fill you with all joy and peace in believing, that ye may abound in hope, in the power of the Holy Ghost*'. In this final benediction it is interesting to observe how its leading words and ideas, '*hope*', '*joy*', '*peace*', are suggested by the quotations given. With '*the God of hope*' cf. '*the God of patience*' (**15**[5]), and '*the God of peace*' (**16**[20]).

To **14**[1]-**15**[13] preachers will naturally turn for guidance in treating the problems of disunity which arise in Christian communities at all times, often connected with secondary issues. One cannot fail to be impressed by the large-minded manner in which Paul handles these problems, and the number and variety of the considerations raised, our common allegiance to the one Lord (**14**[6-9]), our accountability to God (**14**[10-12]), walking in love (**14**[15]), the Kingdom of God (**14**[17]), the insight which faith gives (**14**[23]), not pleasing ourselves (**15**[1-3]), being of the same mind (**15**[5]), glorifying God (**15**[6, 9]), abounding in hope (**15**[13]). Every theme glows.

FIVE

Concluding Explanations and Greetings

15¹⁴-16²⁷. This final part of the Epistle is personal in character. It may conveniently be treated in three sections: (1) **15¹⁴⁻²¹**, Personal Explanations; (2) **15²²⁻³³**, Paul's Future Plans; (3) **16¹⁻²⁷**, Personal Greetings.

(1) 15¹⁴⁻²¹: Personal Explanations

There is an atmosphere of charm and courtesy in these verses which throws a welcome light upon Paul's personality. He compliments his readers on their goodness and knowledge and explains why he has written in view of his sense of a special mission to the Gentiles.

15¹⁴. '*I . . . am persuaded*'. Cf. **8³⁸**. A permanent conviction is expressed. Paul wants to make it clear that although he has admonished them in **12¹-15¹³**, he has no doubts about their goodness, their grasp of the faith, and their ability to instruct one another.

'*goodness*', that is goodness of heart.

'*knowledge*', their understanding of Christian principles.

15¹⁵⁻¹⁶. He writes the more boldly in part by way of reminding them of what they know already, and he does this because of his commission by God's grace to be a minister of Christ Jesus to the Gentiles.

'*a minister*'. The Greek word means 'a priest'.

'*ministering the gospel of God*', that is, 'in the priestly service of the gospel', this ministry consisting in offering the Gentiles as an acceptable sacrifice to God, consecrated by the Holy Spirit. Compare the same use of sacrificial language in **12¹**. In the spiritual sense of the word he is a priest in bringing men to God.

15¹⁷. He can therefore glory in things which belong to God, but '*in Christ Jesus*', that is, in fellowship with Him, in the sphere of things in which He is the centre. See the note on 6¹¹.

15¹⁸⁻¹⁹. The only things he will dare to speak of are those done by Christ through him in speech and in deed, in the power of '*signs and wonders*', in the power of the Holy Spirit.

'*signs and wonders*'. These are two of the terms commonly used in the New Testament to describe miracles, the third being '*mighty works*'. The first Christians were conscious of being able to perform works of a supernatural character, which they attributed to the power of the Holy Spirit. Cf. 2 Cor 12¹². See also 1 Cor 12²⁸ and Heb 2⁴. A '*sign*' is a token of divine power, a '*wonder*' a marvellous act, a '*mighty work*', a deed generally one of healing, wrought by the power of the Spirit. Such acts were regarded as signs of the presence of the Messianic Age. That strange things happened cannot be doubted in view of Paul's testimony, but their precise character can no longer be determined.

'*and round about even unto Illyricum*'. Probably the Roman province is meant on the eastern shores of the Adriatic Sea and missionary labours as far as its borders.

'*the gospel of Christ*', the good news about Him.

15²⁰⁻²¹. '*making it my aim*', '*striving eagerly*', '*being ambitious*' (*RV*m). 'It is my ambition' (*NEB*).

'*not where Christ was already named*', that is, where He has not been heard of, or, possibly, worshipped. He does not want to build on another man's foundation. Cf. Eph 2²⁰, '*the foundation of the apostles and prophets*'. His aim is further described in the language of Isa 52¹⁵. Not a few overseas missionaries have been inspired by Paul's example.

Paul's Christian courtesy, the things he selects for commendation, and the nature of ministerial priesthood are among the subjects suggested by this section.

(2) 15²²⁻³³: Paul's Future Plans

Paul explains that he intends to visit the Roman Christians on his way to Spain after he has first carried to Jerusalem a gift from the Gentile communities for the relief of the poor among the brethren there. He clearly anticipates danger during this visit and asks for the prayers of his readers that he may be delivered from peril and that the offering which he will bring may be acceptable to the Jerusalem community, so that he may come with joy and find rest together with them.

15²²⁻⁴. '*hindered these many times*'. Paul is referring to his missionary labours in Asia Minor, Macedonia, and Achaia, which for many years have delayed the fulfilment of his longing to visit Rome. By '*place*' he means opportunity for missionary work.

'*whensoever I go unto Spain*'. The time is not yet certain. He hopes to see them on his way westwards.

'*to be brought on my way thitherward by you*', that is, to be sent forward by their prayers and good wishes. Cf. 1 Cor 16⁶, 2 Cor 1¹⁶.

'*if first in some measure I shall have been satisfied with your company*'. This rendering is over-literal. Paul is not stating a condition, but naming a time dependent on other events. '*in some measure*' (or '*partially*') courteously suggests that his continued journey (to Spain) must set a term to his enjoyment of their company. Translate, 'when in some degree I have had the enjoyment of your company', or 'when for a while . . .'.

15²⁵⁻⁶. At the present time he is going to Jerusalem ministering, to the saints.

'*ministering*'. The reference is to the Apostolic Collection for the poor at Jerusalem to which Paul attached the greatest importance.

'*the saints*'. See the note on 1⁷.

'*Macedonia and Achaia*'. See the accounts in 1 Cor 16 and 2 Cor 8-9.

15²⁷. The contribution has been prompted by goodwill, but it is also a debt since the Gentiles owed so much to the community at Jerusalem. See the similar argument in 1 Cor 9¹¹.

'*carnal*'. See the note on 7¹⁴. But here, as the contrast with '*spiritual*' shows, the meaning is 'material'. So *NEB*.

15²⁸⁻⁹. When he has accomplished this purpose he will go to Spain via Rome.

'*and have sealed to them this fruit*'. The seal indicates the

owner. See, with reference to baptism, 2 Cor 1[22] and Eph 1[13].
Here Paul may be thinking of the condition laid down at the
Council of Jerusalem, '*only they would that we should remember
the poor; which very thing I was also zealous to do*' (Gal 2[10]).

'*I will go . . . unto Spain*'. Did Paul ever go to Spain? The
evidence that he did so is very inconclusive and many modern
New Testament scholars think that he was executed under
Nero at the end of his period of detention in Rome (Acts
28[30-1]).

Meantime he is sure that he will come '*in the fulness of the
blessing of Christ*'.

15[30-3]. Paul asks for the prayers of the Roman community for
three things; that he may be delivered from danger in Judea,
that the contribution he is bringing may be acceptable to the
Jewish community, and that he may come to Rome in joy,
through God's will and '*find rest*' together with his readers
there.

'*strive together*'. Intense supplication is meant.

'*in joy*'. Cf. 14[17], 15[13].

'*by the love of the Spirit*'. The love which the Spirit brings.

'*acceptable*'. He is not sure that the offering will be received
in its true meaning in Jerusalem as a proof of goodwill.

'*together with you find rest*', that is, rest and refreshment of
spirit.

15[33]. A short benediction closes the section. '*Now the God
of peace be with you all*'. See also 15[13], 16[20b, 25-7]. The fre-
quency of these benedictions is one of the reasons for thinking that fragments of other Pauline letters are to be seen in
15[14-33] and 16[1-23].

'*the God of peace*'. Cf. 16[20]. See the note on 15[13].

The subject of the Apostolic Collection rewards expository treatment, in view of its motives, the importance Paul attached to it, and
the dangers to which it exposed him. The relevant passages are
noted above. See also Acts 24[17].

(3) 16[1-27]: Personal Greetings

The section consists of a brief commendatory letter regarding
Phœbe (16[1-2]), a series of personal greetings (16[3-16]), a warning

against false teachers (16¹⁷⁻²⁰), the greetings of Paul's companions (16²¹⁻³), and a final doxology (16²⁵⁻⁷).

16¹. Letters of commendation were common in the ancient world and especially necessary in the early Christian communities, in order to guard against imposters and to secure a welcome for those away from home. Cf. 2 Cor 3¹.

'*Phœbe*' is otherwise unknown to us.

'*a servant*'. Read 'deaconess' (*RV*m), although it is not certain whether an order of deaconesses existed at this time. Cf. Phil 1¹ ('*deacons*').

'*Cenchreœ*', the port of Corinth, from which city Paul is writing.

16². She is to be received '*in the Lord*', that is, within the Christian fellowship, and in a manner worthy of '*the saints*' (cf. 1⁷) and on personal grounds.

'*a succourer*'. Literally 'a patroness', in the sense of giving hospitality to many and to Paul himself.

16³⁻⁵. '*Prisca and Aquila*'. Prisca (1 Cor 16¹⁹, 2 Tim 4¹⁹), otherwise Priscilla (Acts 18², ¹⁸, ²⁶). She is mentioned first probably as being the more outstanding personality. The two were tent-makers, like Paul, and came from Rome to Corinth when Claudius expelled the Jews from Rome (Acts 18¹⁻²). Later they travelled with Paul to Ephesus where they instructed the learned Apollos in the faith. Here, in **16⁵**, as in 1 Cor 16¹⁹, reference is made to '*the church that is in their house*'. If the chapter belongs to the original Epistle, they must have returned to Rome. In 2 Tim 4¹⁹ they appear to have returned to Ephesus. It is argued by some that the movements of Prisca and Aquila are better explained if Chapter **16** was written for the Church at Ephesus, and further support for this hypothesis is claimed from the fact that Paul is able to send so many greetings to his readers.

'*who for my life laid down their own necks*'. What peril they incurred is not known to us. Some great service during the tumult at Ephesus is a natural suggestion. How great it was is shown by the fact that Paul's gratitude was shared by '*all the churches of the Gentiles*'. It is to be noted that only in this chapter in Romans does Paul speak of '*churches*' or '*the church*' (16¹, ⁴, ⁵, ¹⁶, ²³) in the sense of 'house-church'.

'*Epænetus*' is described as '*my beloved*' and as '*the firstfruits of Asia unto Christ*', that is, the first convert in the Roman province of Asia. Nothing more is known of him.

16⁶⁻⁷. The same must be said of '*Mary*' and of almost all the people mentioned in the chapter.

'*Andronicus and Junias*' are Jews and prisoners with Paul. They had become Christians at an earlier date.

'*of note among the apostles*'. The words '*of note*' mean that the two were outstanding personalities. The phrase is of great importance because it is one of the indications that '*the Apostles*' were a wider body than 'the Twelve'. Paul describes himself as an Apostle (1¹, Gal 1¹, 1 Cor 1¹, 4⁹, 9¹, 2 Cor 1¹, etc.), and the name is applied to Barnabas (Acts 14⁴, ¹⁴), and perhaps to Silvanus (1 Thess 1⁶⁻⁷) in addition to Andronicus and Junias.

16⁸⁻¹⁶. '*Ampliatus*'. A slave name found in the cemetery of Domitilla, one of the earliest Christian catacombs.

'*Urbanus*', a common slave name.

'*Stachys*' is a Greek name.

'*Apelles the approved in Christ*'. See the note on **14¹⁸.**

'*the household of Aristobulus*'. Lightfoot held that these were the former slaves of a grandson of Herod the Great and a friend of Claudius. The next name, *Herodion*, is that of a Jew.

'*the household of Narcissus*'. Narcissus has been identified with Tiberius Claudius Narcissus, a freedman of the imperial house.

'*Rufus*' may well be the man of that name mentioned in Mark 15²¹.

'*his mother and mine*' suggests that she had shown great kindness to Paul. Other women mentioned by Paul are Tryphæna and Tryphosa, apparently sisters and perhaps twins, Persis who is said to have '*laboured much in the Lord*' (or 'so long'), Julia possibly the wife of Philologus, and the unnamed sister of Nereus.

Most of the other names are those of slaves. In sum, they support the Roman destination of the chapter. Asyncritus, Phlegon, Hermes, Patrobas, and Hermas may have formed a group, since they are mentioned along with '*the brethren who are with them*', and the same also may be true of the five

mentioned in verse **15**, '*Philologus and Julia, Nereus and his
sister, and Olympas, and all the saints that are with them*'. Paul
sends greetings to a Church he had not visited in Col 4⁷⁻¹⁸.

'*a holy kiss*'. Cf. 1 Thess 5²⁶, 1 Cor 16²⁰, 2 Cor 13¹².

16¹⁷⁻²⁰. These verses, with their references to false teachers,
are difficult to explain in a letter of Paul to Rome. Apparently
he knows of people who had disturbed the peace of the community. Self-centred and of fair and flattering speech, they
beguiled the hearts of the innocent. Paul wants his readers to
be wise toward that which is good and guileless toward evil;
'*The God of peace*' (cf. **15³³**), he declares, will crush Satan under
their feet shortly, obviously using '*Satan*' in a metaphorical
sense.

For the benediction, '*The grace of our Lord Jesus Christ be
with you all*', see the note on **15³³.**

16²¹⁻³. This postscript gives the greetings of Paul's companions. For '*Timothy*' see Acts 16¹⁻³, 2 Cor 1¹. A '*Lucius of
Cyrene*' is mentioned in Acts 13¹, and a '*Jason*' in Acts 17⁵⁻⁹.
'*Sosipater*' may be the '*Sopater*' of Acts 20⁴. For '*Gaius*' see
1 Cor 1¹⁴, Acts 19²⁹. A '*Gaius of Derbe*' is mentioned in Acts
20⁴.

'*Tertius*', Paul's amanuensis, adds his greetings. In Acts 19²²
reference is made to an '*Erastus*' (along with Timothy). He
may be '*the treasurer of the city*' mentioned here. Of '*Quartus
the brother*' nothing is known.

Verse **24,** which is a repetition of **20b,** is omitted by the
best MSS.

16²⁵⁻⁷. The best MSS have this final doxology in its present
place, but one MS, with some support, omits the passage, a
few have it at the end of Chapter **14,** and a few others in both
positions. In view of its vocabulary and ideas it is widely,
but not universally, held to have been added at the time when
the Pauline letters were collected to form a group. Moffatt
encloses the passage in brackets.

'*the preaching*'. Cf. 1 Cor 1²¹.
'*according to my gospel*'. Cf. **2¹⁶.**
'*the revelation of the mystery*'. Cf. 1 Cor 2⁶, ⁷, ¹⁰, Eph 3³⁻⁶.
The distinctive phrases, while Pauline in the broader sense,

have a later ring: '*the mystery which hath been kept in silence through times eternal*' (cf. Col 1[26-7], 2[2-3], Eph 3[5. 9]; also 11[25], 1 Cor 2[7]), '*the scriptures of the prophets*' (cf. 3[21]), '*according to the commandment of the eternal God*' (cf. 1 Tim 1[1], Titus 1[3]), '*obedience of faith*' (cf. **1**[5]), '*the only wise God*' (**11**[33], cf. 1 Tim 1[17]).

'*to him that is able to stablish you*'. Cf. Eph 3[10]. '*stablish*', better '*strengthen*'. This is the basic idea in the doxology.

'*to whom be the glory*'. The ascription is to God.

The homiletical suggestiveness of the chapter appears in the manner in which Paul refers to his friends, always a revealing characteristic. Further, the promise, '*The God of peace shall bruise Satan under your feet shortly*', has modern significance, reminding us, as it does, that '*Satan*' is used in many senses, and is not only the name of a personal devil; '*Shortly*' implies that God has His own time, and it is highly significant that He acts as '*the God of peace*'. It takes a '*God of peace*' to shatter '*Satan*'! Finally, we cannot fail to notice how deeply rooted divine strengthening is, based in the gospel and the preaching of Jesus Christ, reaching back to times eternal, manifested in the scriptures according to God's command, and made known to all nations with a view to the obedience that springs out of faith. Our spiritual resources are found in the atmosphere of worship, and they cannot be over-estimated.